and baby makes three

self care for new parents

by
carol n. kanter

the apocryphile press
BERKELEY, CA
www.apocryphile.org

To Jodi and Wendy

For all the special feelings of being a parent

apocryphile press
BERKELEY, CA

Apocryphile Press
1700 Shattuck Ave #81
Berkeley, CA 94709
www.apocryphile.org

First published by Winston Press, 1983.
First Apocryphile edition, 2007.
© 1983 by Carol N. Kanter.
ISBN: 1-933993-27-8

Cover photo: Tone Stockenström

This publication is designed to provide accurate and
authoritative information in regard to the subject matter
covered. It is sold with the understanding that the publish-
er is not engaged in rendering medical or other professional services. If expert assistance or counsel is needed,
the services of a competent professional should be sought.

Printed in the United States of America.

Acknowledgments

This book is the offspring of many caring and nurturing people.

Mrs. Bianca Gordon has been a source of professional and personal wisdom, support, and inspiration for me since 1967-68, when she was my mentor at Anna Freud's clinic in London. My interest in infants and parents has been strongly shaped by her influence.

More directly, my friend and colleague, Dr. Marilyn Susman, helped me formulate the outline of chapter headings for this book. She gave me the push I needed to begin to write.

I am indebted to Dr. William Filstead for his teaching of qualitative research methods; to Dr. Phyllis Loeff for helping me design and implement a seminar for new-parent couples; to Dr. Eitan Schwarz for his generous investment of time and expertise in coleading follow-up seminars with me and encouraging my writing; to Highland Park Hospital, and especially to members of the Department of Psychiatry, for their interest, acceptance, and support of this program of seminars, "Project Family Circle."

I am grateful to my earliest readers for their useful critiques. Each of them has made a special contribution to the final form of this work—my parents Dr. and Mrs. Robert and Rae Nussbaum, Jodi Kanter, Susan and Dick Kiphart, Maxene Oshinsky, Marsha Freed, Phyllis Segal, Ken Manaster and Sandy Fox, Dr. Cindy Thompkins, Dr. Janis Mendelsohn, Steffa Mirel, Dr. Sherman Feinstein, Dr. Alan Schnaiberg, and Dr. Bernard Beck. Special appreciation goes to my friend Michael Oberman who, with the assistance of Mary Culhane, typeset my manuscript for submission to publishers. Michael Leach of Continuum Press was instrumental in my persisting to find a home for this book and in my submitting the manuscript to Winston Press, where Lois Welshons was my very helpful editor.

To the ten new parents who agreed to talk with me so openly and for so many hours about their experiences, I want to express my sincere appreciation. I hope they will feel personally gratified at the significant contribution each has made.

My sister and friend, Mrs. Julie Heifetz, a pediatric counselor and a writer, read my pages with a great deal of thought and expertise. Her suggestions made important contributions to the specific content of these chapters. I am grateful to her.

And finally, my husband, Arnie Kanter, has read and reread this work in all of its successive stages. For all his none-too-gentle criticisms, it has been his interest, his basic conviction that this book is worth doing and reading—not to mention his assistance as a writer—that have motivated this effort.

Carol N. Kanter

Contents

BABY'S NEEDS

What's Going On Here?

Poof! You are parents.

You decided to have a baby, and you witnessed the magic of your baby's birth.

The process of deciding on, expecting, and having this baby may have seemed endlessly long or breathlessly short; uncomfortably difficult or remarkably easy. In any case, after a pregnant pause, suddenly you are parents. A new person has appeared and, amazingly enough, has come to live with you.

How does it feel to you, this happening, this new family status? Your answer may differ depending on how soon after delivery you are asked this question and on how the pregnancy, labor, and delivery went for you. Your answer may also vary depending on countless other factors, such as:

—how much sleep you have been losing,

—how closely what you are going through approximates what you expected,

—how long it took you to conceive,

—how definite you felt about the sex your baby should be and which sex actually came along,

—how much—or how little—experience with babies you have had in your life,

—how much support you are currently getting from others in your life (particularly from your partner, your baby's other parent),

—how easily your baby can be comforted at this stage of life,

1

—how healthy your baby is,
—how you have felt in the past about yourself as a
  caretaker,
—how you yourself were parented,
—how much you think or feel you are having to give up
  of your pre-baby self and life,
—how much pleasure you are getting from your baby
  and your new role as a parent.

In short, how it feels to have a first baby is a very complicated question indeed. Your responses probably represent a "mixed bag" of comfortable and uncomfortable feelings, each of which seems to take on a different weight at different times. The combination of all your emotional reactions can be confusing—even overwhelming—particularly since your own emotions are clearly not the only focus of your attention at this point. There is, after all, this little person whose needs you must tend to, this baby who is so surprisingly adept at taking up so much of your waking hours, not to mention some of your would-be sleeping hours.

A crying baby, as you well know, is an insistent little creature. And even when not crying, a newborn makes demands on your time, energy, and ingenuity. After all, a noncrying baby can be fun to play with, and you feel you surely ought to take advantage of those opportunities, right? All of which leaves precious few moments for stepping back to consider exactly how this parenting feels to you. How do you feel about being a new parent, beyond just plain tired?

Since you are reading this book, parenting must be of special interest to you—and probably still a rather new endeavor. Yes, it's true that parenting will seem new to you each time your child enters a new phase or age, which of course will happen continually. But right now this parenting business is absolutely new, possibly overwhelmingly new. And nothing—neither pregnancy nor labor—nor, for that matter, classes, or books, or even past experiences—could have adequately prepared you for all the newness now around you. With all the changing emotions and the newness you're experiencing, you are unlikely to be feeling completely at ease and positive about how you're doing in this role. Vague doubts about parenting are certainly common among new parents, but they are rarely discussed openly and often not acknowledged at all. Usually new parents talk instead about more upbeat aspects of their parenting, like their baby's weight gains (that is, how well they are feeding the baby), their baby's different cries (that is, how well tuned in they are to the baby's signals), or their baby's developmental "milestones" (that is, how appropriately they are stimulating and responding to the baby). This kind of reassurance is important, but it can discourage the open sharing of more troublesome feelings and concerns, which all too often then become out-of-bounds subjects.

The problem is that when negative feelings about being a parent are avoided, the feelings themselves begin to seem so scary that they tend to take on proportions of the "unspeakable." Unattended, these troublesome feelings require more and more energy to keep quietly inside. And this leaves you less energy for the more constructive aspects of parenting.

Thus, however comfortable or uncomfortable your various feelings may be, they deserve your respectful attention. Unfortunately, it's neither automatic nor easy to examine your own complex set of responses to parenting your new baby. It's particularly hard to do such examining alone. So perhaps you can use this book to help you recognize and sort through your own feelings as they unfold.

Although your own experience clearly has been, is, and will continue to be unique in many ways, there are some responses which many people have in common when they become first-time parents. If you realize that your experience is similar to what other new parents have encountered, you probably will feel less alone, better able to accept and deal with your feelings. So this book will be introducing you to what ten other new parents have experienced, hoping to offer you safe company as you consider what it really does feel like to be a new parent.

Of course, not all of their experiences and feelings will be like yours. Some will seem more familiar than others. It is not a matter of what you "should" or "should not" feel. The descriptions are intended as neither suggestions nor admonitions regarding what you should feel; rather, they are meant to encourage you as new parents to pay attention to yourselves—as individuals and couples—as well as to your baby.

Much of *And Baby Makes Three* deals with how it feels to be a parent. The last part presents a picture of the physical and emotional needs of the third member of your new family—your baby—especially as they relate to your responses and nurturing tasks.

You may well consider questions about what to do for your baby (and when) to be the meat of the matter, the main course. At least, when you think about whose needs come first—Father's, Mother's, or Baby's—doesn't it seem to come down to whoever happens to be screaming loudest at the moment? Well, the most regular screamer of the three of you probably is your baby. So after you read the next two chapters, which you will need for some background, you may be eager to skip ahead to the Baby's Needs section.

But keep in mind that in order to be giving so much to your baby, you must also be getting for yourself. Your supplies are not limitless; they need continual replenishing. So if you do skip ahead, return soon to read the earlier chapters on parent needs. They are not less important. In fact, it is necessary for you to give careful attention to the matters they discuss, or this book—and, more important, your whole parenting experience— would be incomplete, unsatisfying.

Parents' Needs—
As Individuals and as a Couple

Mama Myths and Papa Myths

You are surrounded by some insistent myths about how you should be and what you should feel as a new parent. These myths are so prevalent that they are almost unavoidable. They pass along dangerously contagious beliefs which can affect you without your even realizing that they're around or that you are a believer. The myths prescribe:

—specific roles you should and should not take with your baby,
—particular routes by which you can and cannot arrive at being a good parent,
—even certain ways you must and must not feel about yourself if you do not follow these prescriptions exactly.

Now, it's going to be a bit hard for you to accept that you personally believe in these myths. After all, you are literate, aware, and adult enough to be a parent; certainly you know the difference between fact and fiction. Something extraordinary would have to occur before you would become confused about the distinction and take any myth as gospel.

Well, something extraordinary *has* happened to you—something beyond your having had a baby, as though that alone weren't quite extraordinary enough. With that baby have come extraordinarily strong wishes and intentions on your part to be a good parent. These wishes are so strong, and the way of carrying out your intentions so unclear, that you are unusually receptive to any available prescriptions about what to do and how to feel with your baby. And myths are readily available.

The myths are stories about what being a good mother or good father is all about, stories you probably would not believe if you were to read them or hear them directly. But they come to you in fragments and in disguise. They are dangerous because, undetected, they interfere with the very task in which you are so entirely invested, the caretaking of your new baby. So it's important for you to take a close look at these myths and strip them of their ability to confuse and trouble you.

The myths had their origins in the biological fact that it is a natural capability of women, and only women, to bear children. This fact has been stretched and twisted into faulty assumptions that raise questions riddled with self-doubts:

—Since giving birth to a baby is possible only for women, shouldn't early caretaking be possible only for women?
—Since having a baby is so natural a capability, shouldn't taking care of a baby also come naturally?
—Since caring for a baby should be natural, shouldn't it come automatically and not require learning or practice?
—Since caring for a baby should be natural, shouldn't it be easy?
—Since caring for a baby should be natural and automatic and easy, shouldn't it be possible to do perfect caretaking?
—Since caring for a baby should be natural and automatic and easy, isn't it a sign of inadequacy as a parent (or worse, as a person) to look around for direction in how to do what and when for your baby?

It's worth your while to think about whether any of the self-doubts that lurk in these questions may have crept unnoticed into your own intentions about being a good parent.

Historically, a "good mother" has been considered one

who gives physical and emotional nurturing, while a "good father" provides financial support. Although at present parenting roles are less clearly defined, the cultural mythology lives on enough that "mothering" is still a synonym for "nurturing," and "provider" still describes the father.

It is important to recognize that parenting roles are not genetic, sex-linked "givens." If you recognize the myths as myths, you will preserve the option of modifying culturally typical roles to fit your own needs and desires. So how might you want to modify your parenting role?

As Father Provider you may be feeling the full weight of financial responsibilities that have been plunked heavily down upon your shoulders. Until recently your family may have had a second source of income. Now there are more expenses and less income. As Provider, you may feel burdened, proud, or simply grown up in some new way.

But if you were content to settle for the historically designated role of Provider, you probably would not be reading a book like this. So you must have some interest in challenging the myth of rigid, historically prescribed parenting roles, in having other kinds of roles as a father in your new family. But what other roles? How much nurturing do you really want to do? How much of an added burden might that be?

As Mother Nurturer, you may be feeling the full weight of the care of your baby resting heavily on your shoulders. In this culturally familiar role pattern you may feel overwhelmed, proud, and/or somehow more complete as a woman. You may want to devote all of your time to your family right now, even though you may worry about what others will think—how you'll feel about yourself—since it has become so popular to be a working mother.

On the other hand, you may wonder what other roles you will be able to fill while being a mother in your new family. Can you do more than take care of this new baby? How much more? Can you indeed return to work and juggle all the demands if you really want or need to do so?

Whatever the ideas you each have about being a father or mother, for at least some time after the baby arrives home, Dad goes back to work to Provide, while Mom stays home to Nurture. This setup feeds directly into the myth that mothers—certainly and automatically—know how to mother and fathers don't. Mom gets long workdays of practice in picking up her baby's cues and learning about her baby's patterns and temperament. Then Dad comes home and marvels at how Mom seems to know just what the baby wants and needs. He may brag to others (including other new parents) about how naturally adept a mother she is. He may even try to keep pace with her "talents." He may become discouraged. Why, there must be something innately maternal about mothers, which fathers couldn't possibly have or develop.

Indeed, there are some biological (and maybe even psychological) "givens," such as the "let-down" reflex in nursing mothers that causes milk to be available in breasts in response to the infant's cry. But genetically sex-linked, programmed responses do not account for how the mother holds, talks to, or even feeds her infant. Whether you are a mother or a father, you will need time and practice to learn about your baby and how to care for him or her.

You agree, right? It makes good sense that anyone (even you) would require both time to get to know a baby (even your own) and practice in responding appropriately to that baby's needs. Even though you agree, you are ready to raise a disapproving eyebrow at yourself anytime you're unsure of just what to do for your fussing or screaming baby. You do so want to be a "good parent."

So watch out for the myths! They can be serious, painful stumbling blocks to your developing self-esteem as a parent. And parenting—"quality" parenting—is extraordinarily important to you.

Your perception of yourself as a parent is now intimately connected with your view of your baby. Therefore, if you bump into some treacherous myth (created by your very own culture) and trip and fall in your own estimation, there is an additional risk: Your good feelings about your baby might be damaged as well. This would be an unhappy accident. You'll want to put an abrupt halt to such myth-induced cycles of feeling "bad parent-bad baby."

Myths about parenting are powerfully sneaky. No one admits to believing their nonsense. No one would say, "Oh, sure, I'm hoping to meet my baby's needs perfectly; I'm hoping to be a Perfect Parent." But somehow there are Perfect Parent expectations loose in this culture that you as a new parent have probably absorbed unawares. They may crouch inside ready to spring out in self-criticism or self-doubt, waiting to gnaw through in feelings of frustration and depletion, disrupting your learning process with vague uncomfortable notions that you really should be better able to handle your own baby's needs and your new parenthood.

Another myth lurks about, secretly challenging your rational self. This myth whispers reminders that caring for a baby ought to be fairly easy. After all, people have been managing to do more than just the begetting part for a good number of generations now. Besides, a baby has only a small fistful of needs:

—to be fed,
—to be changed,
—to be kept warm and safe,
—to be played with,
—to be held and loved.

What parent wouldn't be able to manage such simple tasks? And if your baby seems to cry a lot or at times goes on crying for what seems like forever, what then do you tell yourself this means—shrieks out!—about you as a parent?

It is a myth that caring for a baby is easy. Caring for a baby, particularly in the beginning, does not all come "naturally." At times it is frustrating and stressful. But people don't talk much about these difficulties. The myths dictate that a "good parent" doesn't have such a hard time. So feeling frustrated or stressed or depleted calls into question your own good parenting. And you don't want to admit even the possibility of such a failure. So you don't talk about it.

New parents, then, are left alone to accumulate unspoken worries about their own inadequacies as parents. Their silence about difficulties makes it appear to other new parents as though all were going rather splendidly for them. Thus they themselves quietly contribute to perpetuating the troublesome myth that parenting infants is easy.

The myths bear interrogating and disarming. You'll want to avoid accepting them unquestioningly; you'll need to demand, Who goes there?

Dr. D. W. Winnicott was a pediatrician and child psychoanalyst from England (1896-1971). Among the significant contributions he made is a concept he called "good-enough mothering." He believed that most mothering parents—whether mothers or fathers—are capable of, and in fact generally supply, "good-enough" nurturing.

When you think about it, this "simple" concept vibrates with myth-shattering power. "Good-enough mothering" implies that perhaps perfect parenting is not only impossible, it is also unnecessary. Perhaps a paraphrase is in order here:

You may satisfy some of your baby's needs all of the time.

You may satisfy all of your baby's needs some of the

time.

But you can't satisfy all of your baby's needs all of
the time.

Nor should you.

As a matter of fact, it would be fair to theorize (or, in
a pinch, rationalize) that it is even important for your
baby to begin feeling and expressing some discomfort as
a first step in getting you to offer comfort in such forms
as milk, dry diapers, cuddling, or rest. The idea is to give
your baby opportunities to feel effective in getting his or
her own needs met by stimulating you to supply whatever is needed. So your baby has to do some crying.

Optimal frustration. Now there's a phrase with a catchy
ring to it. But you may well have already found yourself
wondering at times, if not worrying, about how long
you should let your baby cry. Indeed, how do you measure and administer that "optimal" number of milli-ounces
of the formula Frustration that would best promote your
baby's growth?

Baby-ologists have not yet figured out a formula for
dispensing U.F.O.'s (Units of Frustration, to Opti-
mum)—in spite of the fame and fortune that would belong to whoever could solve such a ticklish scientific
puzzle. Meanwhile, you are left without clear guidelines.

There is, though, a built-in safeguard that will help
take care of this "optimal frustration" question for you
and your newborn: You are human. That, of course, en-
sures that you could not be a Perfect Parent. And so you
go ahead and provide what good care you can, since you
can't "spoil" a newborn with "good-enough" parenting.
And because you are bound to be humanly imperfect,
the care you give just might in and of itself turn out to
be "optimally frustrating" to your baby.

So, you can go right ahead and feel free to give your
baby the best care you can—which includes taking care
of yourself and your partnership with your baby's other

parent. Hints on just how to go about such giving and taking are contained in later chapters of this book.

But go easy on yourself. This book is supposed to make life a bit easier, not to give you more hard labor, or additional tasks. So breathe deeply, relax; you needn't push. After all, this book will still be around tomorrow, even the next day.

Meanwhile, try to challenge some of the myths by realizing that:

—*Traditional roles of Mother Nurturer and Father Provider are not genetically fixed and can be modified;*
—*Mothering a baby is not easy;*
—*Mothering is not an automatic set of functions or feelings; it requires time and practice to learn;*
—*Fathers as well as mothers can learn to do mothering;*
—*Learning is a trial-and-error process. Learning to parent will involve making mistakes, being less-than-perfect but good-enough;*

And finally,

—*Since mothering can be learned, it is permissible—indeed, crucial—to look around for guidelines on how to do what and when.*

Your goal, of course, is to avoid unhappy cycles of feelings about yourself and your baby, while setting in motion happier but realistic cycles:

But where do you turn for specific guidelines on baby care? The next chapter considers various possibilities.

It's Bigger Than Both of You

For you to allow yourself actively to look for and make use of some parenting guidelines, you first needed to feel convinced that mothering an infant is not a mythically easy, all-natural, and automatic process. But there is a further obstacle that may get in the way of your seeking out guidance. This isn't so much a cultural myth as a wish you may have had when you were a child. You expressed it silently or out loud: "I want to be a mommy/ daddy when I grow up." Doesn't that mean you now are supposed to be all grown up? Since you have grown up to be a mommy or daddy, don't you assume that you should now be quite self-sufficient, and know exactly how to behave most appropriately and effectively with your baby? Such questions may be especially burdensome if you happen to be one of the increasing number of people who chose to wait to have a first baby until you were older—more grown up—with your career, your relationship with your partner, and your place of residence more firmly established.

Perhaps, though, the important sign that you are indeed grown up enough is not your self-sufficiency, but rather your maturity in being able to recognize, evaluate, and choose among the various sources that may offer you guidance as a new parent. At different times you might consider different persons to be the most approachable or informative or sensible or experienced or encouraging resources. Your own parenting style can selectively combine the guidance available from others:

—family,

—friends, relatives, co-workers, neighbors, passing
  strangers,
—professionals, "authorities,"
—other new parents.

Family. Large and extended families are less common
now than they were, say, in your grandparents' generation. As a result, you are likely to have become a parent
without ever having had an opportunity to observe others caring for babies, let alone to help much in taking
care of a younger sibling or niece or nephew. So now,
without benefit of any apprenticeship, you are expected
if not to master at least to be quickly good-enough at the
art of parenting an infant. Furthermore, your parents,
with their experience in caring for babies, may not be
available to you to offer appropriate guidance (whether
due to unavoidable circumstances, geographic distance,
or by your choice or theirs).

The word "appropriate," of course, is key. Your parents may or may not be your most appropriate mentors.
The choice is yours. Today, in this society, no specific
person is designated as an "appropriate" guide for new
parents in nurturing their newborns. Thus, the vacant
post tends to attract many applicants.

*Friends, Relatives, Clergy, Co-Workers, Neighbors, Passing
Strangers.* As new parents you undoubtedly have already received, are currently being given, and will continue to get a great deal of advice—whether or not you
request or could use it, and sometimes in spite of your
actively discouraging it. Your reaction to these offerings
might be any of a whole range of feelings:

—surprise at the new connection and sense of continuity you feel with members of the older generation;
—comfort in the knowledge that someone cares;
—relief at the thought that somebody might come up
  with a helpful suggestion;
—confusion at the conflicting notions presented to you

(all or none of which might be worth considering);
—hurt at whatever criticism you may think is being expressed by the fact that somebody seems to feel you
need advice.

. You may be especially prone to feel hurt or threatened
by the advice others offer, to assume their offers indicate
that in some way they think you don't know what you're
doing. It would be easy to make such an assumption
since by now you realize that you couldn't possibly have
figured out all of your baby's cues or requirements, or
even your own role as a new parent and as a new-parent
couple.

If you find yourself resenting advice, remind yourself
that babies, by their very existence, stimulate the involvement and interest of others. This beacon quality
that leads others to respond with interest and care is an
important mechanism for a baby's survival. Besides, at
some level everyone is aware of having once been a baby,
too. So it is understandable that people involve themselves with babies. And one form of involvement is to
give advice—which is a good deal easier than the first-
hand parenting role you have gotten yourself into.

Professionals, "Authorities." Take this book, for instance. It would be fair to consider this writing as the
author's way of being involved with your baby through
you as parents. It is not that you warrant criticism, but
that you (along with your baby) are worthy of others'
interest and input as you meet the challenges of beginning your new three-person family.

Of course, you can't rely altogether on this book, or
on any writings by experts on babies, since not one of
them knows and writes only about your particular baby
or about you as particular parents. Whatever you read,
you'll want to try it on for size, measuring it against your
baby, yourself, your own specific situation. Some items
might fit just perfectly; others might need some altering;
and still others would probably never feel comfortable

to you, and you might as well leave them folded up on the shelf.

The point is that you can expect yourselves as parents to have the unique opportunity of knowing your baby better than the good Dr. Spock himself, better even than your own pediatrician does, since you are the ones spending so much time tending, playing with, and simply watching your baby. This is not to suggest that you abandon that trusty latest edition of Dr. Spock; it can stay right there by your bed, by the baby's changing table, or wherever you'll be able to get your hands on it fast, should some specific worry or question arise. It is a useful tool. It is helpful just knowing it's there.

And your pediatrician's guidance and care are obviously essential. Probably you are following your pediatrician's general guidelines. You take your baby for checkups at the prescribed intervals. You are learning to make use of telephone and in-office time to ask the questions you have collected since your last visit. Perhaps you are already practiced enough to approach your baby's doctor armed with notes to defend your memory against the inevitable, innumerable diversions created by having your baby along with you. (Oh, how easy those visits to the obstetrician seem now!) No doubt you listen closely to your pediatrician's answers and suggestions. After all, this is someone who has had years of training and experience, seen many babies, is being paid for expertise about babies. You find it worthwhile to listen.

It is tempting, with no other clearly appropriate guidelines to follow, to try to adhere precisely to your pediatrician's dictates (even if there was no intent to create a dogma). At the same time, you probably can't help but compare your pediatrician's advice with the advice other new parents—friends, relatives, acquaintances—are getting from their pediatricians. And why not compare, whether the comparison leads to confirmation of what you've heard already or to the presentation of alternative approaches? No one person has all the answers for you about your baby and your parenting. Just think: Someone probably referred you to this doctor in the first place, so someone else had at least one important answer for you already.

Other New Parents. Other new parents are not simply sources of confusion; they are also important resources for you. It is reassuring to know that making the transition from being a couple to being a three-person family is no small feat for anyone. Different individuals and couples feel stressed in different ways and have different means of dealing with the new demands. Ideally it would be useful to have contact with couples whose first baby is:

—a bit younger than yours,
—a bit older than yours,
—the same age as yours,

to foster a calming perspective on

—where you've probably just been,
—what you can expect, more or less,
—how you are not all alone at your current stage of new
  parent-ness.

Each new parent struggles to cope. It is helpful to keep that in mind, not exactly because "misery loves company," but because it would be even more unsettling to feel not only adrift, but alone in your boat to boot.

Every transitional period in life stirs up feelings of being at sea. Beginning parenthood is such a time. No longer are you just two persons, a couple. Yet you probably don't yet feel as if you're safely anchored there in the Parenthood Port, either. It is nice to know you are not voyaging alone, especially since the passage is never altogether smooth and is more often than not surprisingly rocky indeed. Call on some of the other passengers. They might not be able to bail you out entirely, but their support can help you stay afloat. Besides, you might feel encouraged to recognize that your support contributes to the buoyancy of others on board as well.

More about support follows. And you will want to give yourself permission to get whatever support you can. After all, it's not easy to maturely and selectively combine the guidance other people offer—choosing what makes sense and feels most constructive to you—as you develop your own style of parenting your baby.

Where Has All the Freedom Gone?

Once upon a time there was a prince and princess. They lived alone together in their tiny castle. And they were happy.

Oh, they each had their separate lives, pursued their own kinds of work and play. Each had special skills, perhaps appreciated but not particularly shared by the other. Each had special friends, perhaps not so appreciated by the other—in addition to the friends they had in common. Sometimes the prince and princess fought with each other. Yet they shared some interests and they spent time together that was very, very important to each of them.

In fact, they looked forward to their nonworking times, when they could be alone together. They would tell each other details over dinner about how their days had gone. On Saturdays they would pitch in and do some of their homemaking tasks together so that these would seem less like chores. On Sundays they would often stay in bed later than usual, "sleeping in," or treating themselves to coffee and the newspaper at leisure, or cuddling up to some lovemaking, undisturbed by the alarm clock or the tiredness that follows a busy day.

The prince and princess would plan to do things and go places together. They would discuss upcoming activities—a concert (they'd need to get tickets ahead of time), a vacation (they'd have to make reservations in advance), a visit with their royal relatives (they'd better prepare themselves a bit for this one!), a dinner at their place for some friends (they'd better invite the guests they want early so they'll be free to come).

But sometimes—and maybe this was the most fun—they would do things on the spur of the moment. Some days when they both got home on time, they would decide all at once to grab a quick dinner and rush off to that movie they'd been meaning to see. Frequently, they'd find themselves in the mood for a long walk, no particular destination in mind, or a short jog, and simply go out for air and exercise.

Once, on a Friday evening, they suddenly felt like going away for the weekend, so they threw some clothes in a suitcase and took off. Being so *free* felt kind of exhilarating—especially since the king and queen in the castles where each of them had grown up had always had oh-so-many rules and schedules to live by. Yes, the prince and princess were happy to be in charge of their own time, their own whereabouts, their own lives.

It seemed like the prince and princess could go on like this quite happily, for quite a long time. Anyway, that's what the two king and queen sets had begun to think. So they began to drop royal hints, questions like "Is your tiny castle still roomy enough for you?" Or "Who will there be to carry on the royal Name?"

The prince and princess found such hints variously sweet, annoying, funny, pathetic, cute, scary, or outrageous. At times they really felt like screaming, "You know, it's none of your business when or if we have a child!" But that's hardly acceptable court manners. So mainly, of course, they either ignored the questions or tried to humor their parents with joking replies in order to avoid unnecessary confrontations.

Time passed. The prince and princess remained unjostled by the proddings of the royal scepters. But one day the young couple got together and, quite freely and

on their own suddenly* agreed to have a royal baby.
And so they did.

* * *

Here the story is supposed to conclude with something
like "And they all lived happily ever after." "They" may
be understood to refer to all three people in this new
royal family, to the seven people in the extended three-
castle development, or even to the entire kingdom, lucky
to be welcoming so lovely an addition to its royal line.

But this story was not intended to be entirely fanciful.
As a matter of fact, it had to break off at the point of
expected bliss because it could hardly go on and tell what
really happened next to this prince and princess whom
you may have grown to rather like or at least to have
understood in some curiously compassionate way. Would
you have wanted to read that this heroic couple suddenly (and this time, suddenly indeed!) found their lives
disrupted? Would you have cared to learn that they no
longer had time alone together—in fact, never seemed
to feel together in those important little ways at all?

Well, perhaps you guessed that this would be the direction the plot would take next anyway. Perhaps you
could have written the following scenario yourself:

* * *

If there is enough money, the prince and princess will
move to a somewhat larger castle. They then will have
been transplanted from their comfortably familiar place

---

*This is an example of poetic license. How such a couple (even one
of royal blood) comes to this agreement cannot be so sudden a happening. For even if you and your partner had not planned on this
pregnancy, you still went through a process of deciding what to do
about this "accident." In fact, the decision to have a baby is the
subject of another chapter, "So You Wanted to Be Parents!"

to a different setting, one which itself will require more work from them—not to mention their new duties of caring for the royal baby.

Even if they haven't moved, the old place looks very different. Baby things are much in evidence. There is a sense of change, a different feel, which may even seem a bit disconcerting.

The prince is very busy with his work and needs to be away more, putting in longer hours on his job. Or maybe it just seems that way to the princess who, at least for right now, is having to stay home instead of going out herself, as had been her habit. And as long as she is around more, she feels she has to take care of more of the castle household tasks by herself. And these now feel more like chores than they used to.

The princess had expected that she would feel tired from having to be up many nights taking care of the baby, maybe even tired from having extra work to do. But she was not prepared for something else she is now strongly feeling: She feels angry. And she feels angry at herself for feeling angry.

The prince, sensing that all isn't going as they had so carefully planned, feels sorry. At times he too feels angry—angry at the princess for being angry; angry at being ignored, replaced as a center of attention, angry at sharing the burden without getting due credit.

He wonders to himself what more he should or could take on his own shoulders. He feels he must evaluate and decide this question alone because there seems to be no time to talk with the princess about this or much of anything else. There seems to be no time even to be together.

Everything is revolving around the royal baby. Dinners no longer occasion the sharing of personal events-of-the-day. Instead, they are orchestrated by, for, and around the mood, timing, and needs of the littlest ruler. When the counterpoint of small cries isn't actually interrupting their meal, the prince and princess are preoccupied anticipating such inharmonic interludes. What conversation does get slipped in is always about the baby and how the *baby's* day had gone. Neither prince nor princess would dare complain aloud about this. After all, they feel proud and lucky to have such a wonderful baby, who is so very, very special to each of them.

But the royal couple are losing touch with each other. His Highness no longer tells Her Highness much at all about his work. He feels that the princess surely has enough on her mind; and besides, his own daily goings-on seem to him rather insignificant by comparison. There is too little time, anyway. Yet he misses the telling and feels a bit sad.

Meanwhile, Her Highness has a nagging sense that she and the prince are growing apart in spite of the special closeness of becoming royal parents together. She feels too tired to try to figure it out right now, but hopes to be able to think and talk about it sometime soon. She too feels a bit sad.

The prince and princess each muse about special times that seem missing now. For instance, their Sunday mornings feel lost to them altogether—at least as distinguished from all the other less leisurely mornings. The royal baby's internal clock does not have an adjustable dial that can be conveniently reset to make the call to arms sound later on Sundays and holidays.

Even more alarming are the changes which have taken place in the royal couple's love-making patterns. The royal physician may have pronounced his no-action sentence: "Thou shalt have no sexual intercourse for six weeks." This proclamation may have appeared so out-of-the-blue to them that they were taken by surprise and did not regain their balance in time to ask the good doctor why. Or under what conditions might the sentence be reduced? No matter; their upbringings probably would have prevented them from posing such indelicate questions anyway. They wonder if most ordinary people know the answers and, embarrassed, choose just to wait quietly for six weeks—or, as quietly, choose not to wait.

The sentence turns out to be somewhat moot, anyway, since Her Highness's interest in lovemaking is not very great. Or perhaps she learned somewhere that this lack of interest is to be expected, and she fears it might be unmaternal were she to admit that she is indeed interested.

In either event, the situation naturally is rather depressing to His Highness. The prince's still-active interest adds further stress to their feelings of being out of step with each other. They are confused about how to continue their physical relationship. There seems to be no appropriate source of information for them. They each silently promise to see to it that this decrease in sexual communication will not matter too much. They think it shouldn't be too hard to keep this promise because they are so tired seemingly all the time now that they mainly feel the urge to go straight to sleep whenever possible. Besides, officially it's only six weeks.

Meanwhile, the prince and princess seem to be uninterested in or incapable of going out alone together, leaving the royal baby in someone else's good care. Who in all the kingdom, they ask themselves, could possibly be trusted with so precious a charge as the royal babe? Anyway, would they really be able to relax and enjoy such time alone, or would they be too worried about what was happening back at the castle?

In a later episode of this tale, Their Highnesses manage to get a loyal caretaker to stay with the royal baby, and they go off to a nearby inn for two hours between feedings. Once again they are alone together. They finally have a chance to catch up a bit with each other. They've both been waiting to share so many thoughts and feelings about what's been going on with them individually and in their relationship. But what do they talk about there at the inn? The little person who has so changed their lives! It seems to require a giant effort for them to pull away, even temporarily, from their baby's powerfully magnetic bonding.

So what hope remains for that spur-of-the-moment type of fun they used to enjoy together? Clearly, such spontaneity is completely out of the question now. In fact, it now seems necessary to plan day-long schedules beginning early each morning, trying to get a running start in order to make time for all the requisite routines.

Even then nothing seems to go as planned. For instance, just when they get ready to take the royal baby with them, say, to visit a friend, the little royal face turns grunting-red, and the diaper must be changed again. By the time the cleaning up has been accomplished, the next feeding is about due. They are forever late. Sometimes they feel hard pressed to get showers for themselves, let alone to feel exhilaratingly *free*.

Their Highnesses know deep down, sometimes way, way deep down, that they are delighted with the royal baby and proud to have become royal parents. But it doesn't quite feel like they've reached the part where "they all lived happily ever after."

∗ ∗ ∗

The story, of course, doesn't end there. In truth, this is only a beginning. You know that because you may have already lived through part of this story yourself, to some extent. By now you and your partner may have become clever at avoiding such royal pitfalls so that you no longer allow them to distance you from each other. Naturally, your relationship can't be just the same as it used to be; it does have a new dimension. But you are finding ways to ensure that this new dimension is more an addition, an asset, than a loss.

It will be some time before your baby will be capable

of relating to both of you at the same moment and truly participating in a three-way relationship. Instead, three rather distinct two-way relationships are optimally under way at this early stage:

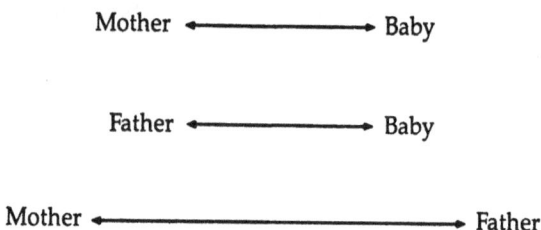

Mother ◄─────────► Baby

Father ◄─────────► Baby

Mother ◄──────────────────► Father

And it is the mother-father dyad that best forms the steadying base of the triangle that will develop:

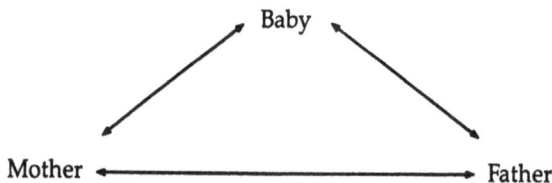

Baby

Mother ◄──────────────────► Father

At some level you realize that it is your relationship with your baby's other parent that must provide the backbone for your new family unit. You also realize that, in the face of all the other demands on your time, energy, and caring, this crucial relationship will require ongoing effort, attention, and monitoring. And you resolve to keep it in mind. So, occasionally you take time to ask yourself such pointed questions as these:

—"What have I managed to share with my partner today—or this week, even—about myself, my own
feelings, *APART FROM OUR BABY?*"
—"What unrelated-to-baby thoughts or feelings or events
has my partner managed to share with me recently?
Did I express my interest?"
—"Am I letting my partner know that the two of us are
still a most important twosome to me? Am I convinced
of that myself?"

It is too easy to put your partnership on hold while
you gain comfort with your new family member and your
new role of parent. However, this active adult relationship is a critical element in the "holding environment"
which you want to provide for your baby—as well as for
yourself. And, hard as it may be to keep the partnership
alive and well, you know that it would be all the harder
to reactivate were you unwittingly to neglect it for too
long.

So you face the fact that there are countless constraints
on the amount of time you have together. And you in-
vest in the insurance of finding ways to compress things
a bit: You go out alone together for two hours rather than
take off for two days. You limit your joint shopping to
one group of stores instead of planning to make stops all
over the place. You engage in less "small talk" and are
quicker to get down to sharing more basic feelings and
thoughts. In the most efficient ways, you learn to keep
in touch.

Your relationship can supply sustenance and support
to each of you. This support takes a variety of possible
forms.

Support can be a sharing of responsibility. It can take
the form of being in charge of, cooperating on, or taking
turns with certain tasks. Or it can mean simply being
available to think through matters together, to be part of

the sorting out and deciding processes.

Support can also come in the form of whatever is familiar: your partner's presence; discussions which still tend to interest you, stimulate your thinking; responses to you as basically the same person, the same partner you were, pre-baby. In other words, it would be most supportive to both you and your partner if your familiar relationship could serve to keep the newness of parenthood from overwhelming you.

Babies are stimulating in their own way. But the stimulation you get from your baby cannot replace the contact you as an adult need with other adults. That would be too much to ask of both your baby and yourself—an unreasonable burden for so small a person as your baby; an unreasonable limitation for so complex a being as yourself.

So if you spend some time reinforcing your relationship with your partner, you both will end up having more available energy for your baby. You'll need all the support you can get to deal with the surprises new parenthood brings. But that's jumping ahead to the next chapter.

Dreams Versus Diapers

You are living in the midst of Western culture. Unless you happen to have your very own Eastern style guru, who has impressed you with the mystic wonders awaiting you in each and every current moment, you probably pay your share of homage to the future. In other words, you make plans.

Where you are in your life did not simply happen to you all of a sudden. Consciously or unconsciously, you anticipated what you wanted to be, where you thought you'd prefer to live, what kind of lifestyle you would find desirable (within the realm called your Reality). Most recently, you made plans to have a baby. And to one extent or another you have tried, and continue to try, to heed the reliable, future-oriented motto: Be Prepared.

Accordingly, in making your decision to become a parent, you may well have tried to imagine and anticipate—both alone and with your partner—how life might be different with a baby around. Would one of you be staying home more? Who? For how long?

Maybe you quickened your social pace a bit (after the first three-month tired spell passed) in a somewhat frenzied effort to squeeze in dates with friends, movies, vacations—a kind of "last fling"—in anticipation of a severe social drought following delivery. Or perhaps you began staying home more, trying to become accustomed to the pattern-to-be. Or possibly you began accumulating names and phone numbers of potential babysitters, to ensure opportunities for diversions later on.

You may have taken a prenatal class in hopes of preparing for labor and birth. In fact, labor and birth may have become a central goal in your mind, a goal for which you were clearly and actively preparing. You may have practiced relaxation and breathing exercises with your partner. You may have visited the labor and delivery rooms (or prepared your own if you planned to have a home delivery). You may have assembled a kit of supplies suggested by others for use in labor.

Perhaps you attended some "how to" demonstrations on changing, feeding, bathing, which were offered in the hospital before you brought your baby home. Maybe you got hold of books that promised some guidance. Possibly you arranged to observe some other new parent's caretaking activities—or even practiced diapering or bathing or burping or holding your friend's or your cousin's new baby.

You probably planned for where your new baby would sleep, once at home. In preparation, maybe you bought or borrowed a crib, a changing table; you fixed up a place for your baby. You may have done some reading or asking around—especially, among other new parents—about what other items would be good to have on hand for your baby. Maybe you checked out which local drug stores have night hours and/or a delivery service for items you forget or run out of or choose not to buy in advance (perhaps because you do not expect your baby to need, say, a pacifier or liquid aspirin).

You may or may not have been aware of the various expectations you had about your baby and your parenting experience. In any case, you have probably already encountered some surprises, enough to suggest that other surprises lie ahead. And in some instances the expectations you had seem quite important to you. The surprises then can feel seriously upsetting, even dream shattering. Disappointed early expectations can interfere with your developing and maintaining basic positive feelings essential to the emotional wellbeing of you and your new family. In order to protect your embryonic positive feelings about your baby and yourself as a parent, you must be able to adjust your expectations to the innumerable surprises of beginning parenthood.

Many things about parenthood may already have surprised you. In your new role you may have had some general surprises about:

—the weight of the responsibilities,
—the constancy of the needs and tasks,
—the amount of time required of you,
—the permanency of parenthood,
—the loss of no longer belonging to the youngest generation.

These surprises would be worth your thinking about to give yourself a chance to get used to them a bit.

But you've also encountered other, more specific surprises. Thinking about these can bring to light some of the expectations or dreams that you have had. Just as it is important to recognize and debunk the cultural myths about early parenting that you looked at in "Mama Myths and Papa Myths," so too it is important to unmask your own personal expectations. Then they, too, will have less chance of interfering with your good-enough parenting.

One example of a surprise may have involved a specific expectation of importance to you. It may have come with the typical announcement made upon your baby's arrival: "It's a boy!" or "It's a girl!" (Even if an amniocentesis had been performed and you knew the sex of your baby ahead of delivery time, this announcement was an important confirmation for you.) Had you expected or wanted to hear that your baby was the other sex?

How unfashionable such an attitude seems today! It's far more socially acceptable to claim that you never cared whether you had a boy or a girl, so long as it is healthy. But just think how you would have felt if your baby were delivered and your doctor had said, "Well, we don't know if it's a boy or a girl, but it is healthy."

In some instances, people try to convince everyone, most of all themselves, that they really have no particular preference, when in fact the sex of their baby matters to them a great deal. (Surely this is more often the case than could be proven by listening to what people say out loud.) In such instances one is tempted to deny the expectation even to oneself, and to try to cover up any dream-shattering surprise at the disappointing news. However, it's just this sort of coverup that can bottle up emotions inside, where they gain pressure, bubble out in perplexing or inappropriate reactions, and often block essential positive feelings toward one's baby—or toward oneself as a parent.

There are alternatives more constructive than such attempts at denial. Perhaps it would be interesting—indeed, useful—to think about just why you may have wanted a boy or a girl in the first place. As a matter of fact, it's as worthwhile for you to consider this question, if your wish *did* happen to come true, as if you were disappointed in what sex came along. Whatever your wishes, the sex of your child has some specific meanings for you. So you might want to consider the following:

If you wished that your child would be the same sex as you are,

—Might this be because you thought you would have an easier time understanding this new person? Might you be tempted to assume that your baby is so much like you that you can automatically know your chip-off-the-old-block's needs, feelings, talents, flaws? Shouldn't you continually check out your assumptions against your real-life child?

—Or did you wish for a baby of the same sex because you thought your child would be or would accomplish what you have long wished to be or do yourself? Can a brand new individual thrive under so large a burden?

—Were you hopeful that this sameness would ensure the close relationship you want to have with your child? Was the relationship you had with your parent of the same sex more comfortable than the one you had with your other parent? Since your baby's other parent is the opposite sex, do you think your comparative discomfort with your opposite-sexed parent and your expected alliance with your baby might result in some tension between you and your partner now that you are parents? Could you monitor such stress between you and your partner, given its often sneaky and disguised way of entering a relationship? (More about such setups in a later chapter, "Once Upon Your Moms and Dads.")

If, on the other hand, you hoped that your baby would be of the opposite sex from you,

—Was it because you were concerned about being able to remain separate from your baby, fearing you might somehow get "too close"? If so, might you have a tendency to protect yourself—or your newborn—from being "too close" whatever your baby's sex? And how, then, will you be free either to allow your attachment to your baby or to foster your baby's bonding to you?

—Or maybe you anticipated that a child of the opposite sex would offer less competition for your partner's attention and affection?

—Or perhaps you felt that with a child of the opposite sex you might be less tempted to automatically repeat the relationship patterns your own parents had with you? (Again, check out "Once Upon Your Moms and Dads.")

—Or maybe your own relationship was better with your opposite-sexed parent?

When you really think about it, many possible factors weigh in favor of your having *either* a boy or a girl.

In any event, it is not necessary or helpful to try to accept the popular attitude that you don't care, if indeed you do. It would be more useful, require less energy, and be less disruptive to you and your new family, if you admitted to yourself that maybe your baby's sex does matter to you. Certainly it has special meanings for you. Why not try to figure out what those meanings are? Wouldn't that give you a better chance to build on the strengths implicit in those meanings and minimize the effects of the limitations, the dream-shattering aspects of the surprise?

Now, what about the possibility of being surprised in your "as long as it's healthy" expectation? The baby's health is a primary focus of concern for parents-to-be. Worrying about this is another attempt to prepare yourself—in this case, for any health problem your baby might chance to have, so that the surprise won't be so devastating. So after you got the news about your baby's sex, you probably checked for obvious signs that your baby was healthy. The doctor's assurance on this score was necessary but not sufficient by itself. You and your partner needed to check for yourselves that—incredibly!—your combined genetic assembly plants worked efficiently and produced a body with all the necessary parts, the standard equipment.

You counted your baby's fingers and toes. You looked over the telltale boy or girl features as closely as you dared. You almost held your breath to protect yourself from discovering any surprises in the baby's mental or physical makeup. For you knew that your worrying would not have really prepared you had there been anything critically wrong.

Your basic wish for your baby to be perfectly healthy makes you particularly vulnerable. Any surprise in this department is bound to feel altogether dream shattering.

Now, ask yourself quite candidly if you understood this reference to your baby's "perfect" health to mean "good-enough" health. If you did, you have definitely caught the drift. If you failed to make this modification, you are

—probably right in the mainstream,
—perhaps more honestly reflecting your actual response,
—now, hopefully, all the more impressed with just how strong a desire and need you have for your baby to be in *perfect* health.

But perfection here, as elsewhere, is a rarity, if not an impossibility. There are, of course, some relatively rare major health problems that are life-threatening to newborns and may have lifelong repercussions for this new person, and consequently for you as well. If you are having to face such a stressful situation, you will need extra support. It is imperative that you get the help you need. (See the chapter, "Who Cares About Parents, Anyway?")

If your baby has serious health problems, even if you somehow made it through the initial crisis, there is a high probability that your attachment process will have been interrupted. How could you expect to be free to become attached to a baby you fear might not live? Is such an expectation appropriate when you need to prepare yourself for this awful possibility by not becoming too attached? You have to take care of yourself, too, you know.

Alternatively, you could go to the other extreme. In an effort to deny the unthinkable, your attachment to your at-risk baby could so intensify that, later, developmentally appropriate separation could be a problem. (See the chapter "Growing Separately Together.")

So if your baby is at risk, you cannot expect to be able to form an appropriate attachment without professional help. Healthy attachment cannot be forced. If you receive competent professional help, it will not feel intrusive. It will attempt neither to push an interrupted attachment process along in spite of all odds nor to pull

asunder an intensified attachment. Rather, professional
support will offer protection against your becoming totally overwhelmed, so that attachment can later occur
appropriately—after the baby is out of danger, after some
mourning has taken place for the loss of the wished-for
perfectly healthy baby, or even with the next baby in this
family.

"Good-enough" health, however, refers to lesser
problems. The difficulty here is that when these occur,
they may not seem so "lesser" to you. It is difficult to
keep perspective. Please keep in mind that you are in a
particularly vulnerable position. And everything seems
to be monumentally important, critically surprising. Try
to take into account your doctor's assessment that the
problem is:

—minor,
—common,
—likely to heal, disappear,
—correctable,
—threatening neither to life nor limb in the long run.

If this assessment makes sense to you, you can be calmed
and comforted. Then in turn, you will be better able to
calm and comfort your baby.

Well, anyway, there you were in the delivery room,
taking in the news, "It's a girl!" or "It's a boy!" and
checking out your baby's apparent health. Then you really
looked at your baby for the first time. Your first glances
took in the general shape of that tiny body and the facial
features. Perhaps you were surprised at how much uglier your newborn seemed, compared to what your mental picture had promised.

When you had thought ahead about having a baby,
you may have pictured an alert, smiling, cooing, Ivory-
soap-type baby. Chances are that you had not imagined
the red and wrinkly, completely dependent, utterly
helpless, and, moreover, minimally responsive bundle

of potential that actually appeared.

If you found the real-life version uglier than your mental picture had been promising, the surprise may have felt dream shattering. First, the difference between how you had expected your baby to look and how your baby initially appeared to you can raise in your mind the more general question of whether this new child has come equipped to live up to your expectations.

Second, surprise about your newborn's looks may block the strong "parental" emotions that you probably had been expecting—that surge of fatherly or motherly emotion that is supposed to well up automatically from deep inside you at the very sight of your newborn. Such emotions aren't exactly or purely mythical. Some parents do experience such stirrings from the moment they spy their new baby. Some try to fake it or exaggerate what they do feel, because the expectation has reached mythical proportions. Wouldn't anyone truly "cut out" to be a good parent surely experience these nurturant impulses from the very beginning?

Well, from experience you know that it takes awhile to form deep attachments, and that attachments grow and mature over time. You may even be able to admit that your partner has in some ways been different from what you expected. No matter how long and well you knew this person before entering couplehood, most likely your partner proved to be both more and less than you had anticipated. The surprises were most likely mild enough though to be interesting rather than dream shattering or overwhelming. You have come to respect your partner's strengths over time and to cope with your partner's weaknesses. Perhaps you recognize that you may have offered a few surprises to be coped with as well, and you may feel grateful that your partner is coping. You are not a worse partner because, as you have come to these realizations, your relationship has grown over time.

So why couldn't you as a new parent accept that you can come to feel positively enthusiastic, deeply attached to your baby—essentially fatherly or motherly—more gradually than you had anticipated and still be a good-enough parent? Why should a sudden, immediate surge of positive emotions within the first minutes after your baby's birth be any more valid or desirable than the cumulative sense of attachment to and pride in your baby and your new role as a parent that develops over the first days or weeks of your baby's life?

The crucial factor is that attachment does happen. Sooner or later—but not too much later—it should occur. You and/or your partner must experience an attachment to your baby. Only then will your baby be able to form and keep that reciprocal attachment to a mothering person, to experience that "primary bonding" that is essential for his or her normal emotional development. Human attachment, then, is a mutual arrangement.

In baby animals this attachment or "imprinting" has been found to be a capacity specific to a limited time period during the first days of life. Beyond this early critical period the capacity for forming primary attachments seems to be lost. There is no proof that in human babies attachment capacities disappear as early or as completely as they do in animals. But it does seem that bonding in human infants takes place more quickly and easily when it happens relatively early. Therefore, if after a few weeks neither you nor your partner feels especially attached to your baby as his or her primary caretaker, something is seriously amiss.

But caution: Do *not* jump to the conclusion that this means that you are either a bad person or a bad parent. It doesn't even mean that you are incapable of becoming a good-enough caretaker. It just means that something—possibly a dream-shattering surprise—is getting in your way, blocking the unfolding of a natural process. It warrants concern and immediate attention. You cannot count on so fundamental a block going away by itself. And you can't afford to wait too long to see if it does.

The previous two paragraphs may have come to you as something of a surprise in themselves. Certainly they don't convey to you a sense of "There, there. Everything will be just fine." And actually, they are intended to jolt you a bit, to cause you to stop and consider the serious consequences of too lengthy a delay in your baby's forming an attachment to a mothering person.

Chances are that such a lengthy delay in beginning attachment does not apply to you and your baby. But if it does—and this is not so uncommon an occurrence at that—you should deal with this now, while your baby still has full capacities for developing primary bonds. You can consult the chapter "Who Cares About Parents, Anyway?" for suggestions as to what you might do right away to save yourself not only much time and energy but some predictable emotional pain later on.

If you have questions about your baby's attachment to you or your partner as the primary mothering person(s)—or if you simply have some curiosity about how you "just know" that the bonding is going well—you might want to check on it. Of course, you can't simply ask your baby, "How's the attachment going?" But since the process is a reciprocal one, you and your partner can check on it from the other direction, by asking the following questions:

—Do I feel supportive toward my baby? Am I apt to spring forward reflexively if I feel my baby might be in some sort of danger? Am I quick to hear my baby cry?

—Do I feel a sense of satisfaction when I know I meet my baby's most basic needs, most of the time?

—Do I spend time holding my baby, and enjoy this contact?

—Do I spend time looking directly into my baby's eyes, especially during moments between crying and sleeping, when my baby is in that "quiet, alert" state? Do I enjoy this holding of each other's attention?
—Do I, in general, feel proud of my baby?
—Do I feel my baby is responsive to me?

The goal is not to be able to answer "Yes!" to all of these questions all of the time. After all, a healthy attachment is also determined by being able to separate from your baby at appropriate times. So a hovering overprotection, which would prevent your baby from feeling safe when you are not right there, is counter-productive. Healthy attachment conveys to your baby assurances of a very basic safety, not ever-impending anxieties about the possibility of your being physically absent.

Now and then you may need to tiptoe into your sleeping baby's room when you've heard not a peep from that direction in awhile—just to make sure your baby is still breathing. You may feel overprotective or silly about doing this, but it's fine to make sure you get the reassurance you need so long as this is essentially not disrupting your baby's patterns. Naturally, you should take a good hard look at yourself if you find that you not only tiptoe in to take a peek but also wake your baby up each hour to make sure no out-of-the-blue coma has set in.

In any event, if your responses to the above attachment checklist were largely nos, you would be wise to give serious thought, *now*, to what might be getting in your way. Have you run up against one or more dream-shattering surprises? And do get some professional help with this thinking.

Now, to return to the more normal situation: Your baby's basic emotional requirement is for one caretaking person to be available, offering attachment, responding to the baby's need to form a primary bond. One such constant person will do, from the baby's standpoint. But "constant" means that the caretaker is almost certain to remain available and attached to the baby throughout the developmental years. The mother, or the mothering father, could best meet this requirement. So if your partner is filling that need, you could consider yourself off the hook.

However, if you are not forming an attachment to your baby, you may feel excluded from your partner's attachment to your baby on the one hand, or from your baby's attachment to your partner on the other hand. It might be useful to keep in mind that the earliest all-consuming intensity of the mothering person's attachment to the baby is normal and necessary; but it is a temporary state and should gradually become more moderate in degree. Attachment to one's baby does not, cannot replace the adult relationship with one's partner, the baby's other parent.

If you are feeling left out of your baby's attachment to your partner, it may be that you have been surprised by wishes for more firsthand involvement with your baby than you had expected to want. The plans you had made about dividing up caretaking roles—whether you made these alone or with your partner—can be modified. You, too, can feed your baby. You don't have to become a second primary caretaker unless you choose to do so. But giving some bottles yourself during your baby's first weeks is an effective means of promoting your baby's attachment to you as well as to your partner.

Indeed, babies are *capable* of becoming attached to more than one person. So, again, you wouldn't have to take over primary caretaking responsibility if you were to offer yourself as an additional person to whom your baby could become attached. Nor would you be superfluous. You are different from anyone else who may be relating to your baby, and therefore the nature of your relationship, the particular brand of your initial attachment, will be unique. This can help your baby learn early to differentiate people from each other in more subtle ways than simply familiar-and-safe as opposed to unfamiliar-and-unsafe.

From your standpoint, the special, early attachment you could experience with your baby would itself be ample reward. It can be a healthy antidote to all the diapers.

The diapers, that is, the reality of your baby, need not spoil the dreams you have. But as you unmask expectations hidden in your dreams about your baby and yourself as a new parent, you must keep reminding yourself to adapt your dreams to your child, instead of trying to mold your child to fit the dreams.

A Lifeline

In the last chapter, you were invited to think about the plans and preparations you made, the expectations and wishes you harbored, as you approached parenthood. What you anticipated, eagerly or anxiously; what you did, constructively or busily; what you felt, proudly or self-consciously—all may have seemed very new to you. After all, you've never been a parent before. Yet parenthood—and life—are events that do have a past. Your happenings all have a history. No matter how little you consciously prepared for the future or whether you were aware of the contributions of earlier occurrences and perceptions, they nonetheless have shaped where, who, and how you are today.

If you can see and feel that you as a new parent are in some important ways like you were before parenthood set in, then *everything* won't feel so new about your current predicament. You are, after all, the same person and so have good reason to see yourself as a constant in the equation:

$$\text{YOU(Back Then)} + \text{Time}_{\text{past}} = \text{YOU(Now)}$$

The problem is that parenthood, your current lifestyle, relationship patterns, and emotional states may all seem so new that you feel you've taken something of a quantum leap. It seems an even greater leap to come to see yourself as the constant in another stabilizing equation—one that has a future orientation:

$$YOU(Now) + Time_{future} = YOU(Yet\text{-}To\text{-}Be)$$

So you may question whether together these two simple equations will suffice to place your present situation in perspective. Perhaps formulas from higher mathematics may seem necessary to help you make sense of what has happened in your life. Not so.

What may help, though, is a 3-D perspective, a more solid geometry. It is difficult to get a rounded view of anything from close range. It would help you gain perspective if you could step back a bit, get out from under all the diapers. The trick is not to avoid the realities of parenting, but to understand and deal with what's happening in your life. You need to be able to combine the above equations and begin to get a picture of yourself as situated solidly, or at least balanced comfortably, on the continuum of your life:

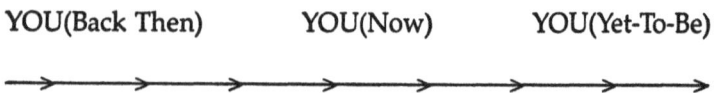

YOU(Back Then)   YOU(Now)   YOU(Yet-To-Be)

$\longrightarrow\!\!\!\longrightarrow\!\!\!\longrightarrow\!\!\!\longrightarrow\!\!\!\longrightarrow\!\!\!\longrightarrow\!\!\!\longrightarrow$

The idea is that if you can get a clear perspective on YOU(Back Then), YOU(Now) will seem less surprising, more familiar; and YOU(Yet-To-Be) can be anticipated more calmly.

As a new parent, YOU(Back Then) includes the particular events that led to your baby's arrival—labor and delivery, pregnancy, and your decision to have a baby—and even your impressions of how your own parents related to you when you were young. YOU(Now) have been shaped by all these past experiences. So to make sense of your present situation and to get more comfortably balanced on the continuum of your life, it would help to have a focused look at your unique history.

The chapters that follow will guide you backwards in time through those pivotal experiences in your history that are most directly related to your parenthood. You may come to see how those earlier experiences helped shape your reactions as a parent. Though beginning parenthood feels incredibly new to you, you are likely to perceive and deal with your new parenthood in ways typical of your unique personality. Your present approach to parenting your baby will therefore echo the ways in which you thought and felt and dealt with earlier events in your life; it will echo your former efforts to make sense out of unfamiliar situations.

By exploring pivotal times in your history, you may be able to evaluate which of your earlier attitudes and behaviors were useful and which disruptive. The goal is twofold: for you to be able to repeat the useful patterns with a greater sense of comfort, confidence, and calm; and for you to be able to modify previously disruptive patterns.

But reflecting on one's own past experiences does not involve simply a nostalgic skip down Memory Lane. Personal reflection that aims at being constructive is no simple task. Besides, exploring what has helped to shape your early parenthood will be tough going partly because your active participation will be required.

However actively you participate in this exploring, though, you may find it difficult to be objective about yourself and your past, all alone. Exploring your past patterns of feeling and behaving might be easier if you could compare them with the similar or contrasting past experiences of other first-time parents. Accounts of other new parents could

—help give you some perspective on your own experience;
—confirm your hunches that in certain ways you've been coping
  —as well as can be expected,
  —much like others in your situation,
  —remarkably well, under the circumstances,
  —not as well as you'd like,
  —not as well as you think might be possible for you;
—encourage you to experiment with some alternative attitudes or approaches;
—suggest some alternative guidelines for you to try out, as is, or adjust to suit your particular requirements;
—offer you good company and the reassurance that *no one* has foolproof formulas on how to parent a baby.

So stay tuned. You are hereby cordially invited on a guided tour of your own Pre-Parenthood. And you're about to have company.

Hello, Folks!

Here to join you on your personal tour of the recent past are ten other new parents. Your tourmates' stories can help you gain perspective on some pivotal experiences in your own past.

These new parents represent quite a wide range of personal styles and relationship patterns, and they all have agreed to share their experiences with you. (These accounts are taken from in-depth interviews with real new-parent couples. These people reappear in later chapters, so if you wish further particulars on who they are in real life, see the chart on p. 165.)

Before, during, or after you read this chapter's capsule versions of your tourmates' stories, you and your partner may each want to answer for yourself the questions that follow each story. If each of you answers independently, and then you both make time to share your perceptions with each other, you might find that the dialogue:

—confirms your former impressions,
—adds an interesting, different perspective,
—supplies new pieces of information for you to consider,
—encourages you to further discussion.

In any event, answering the questions will be good practice in making time to be with each other and in maintaining communication about yourselves. Moreover, the answers to these questions are important. They will tell you a lot about yourself, your style, your relationship with your partner. And they could present opportunities for you to make some alterations in your approaches to

your baby and your experience of parenthood. Your answers are important enough that you might care to write
down or tape record them as you go along to make it
easier to give further consideration to your responses,
both alone and together with your partner.

* * *

I. Barb and Bob can be characterized as a rather "traditional" couple in their marriage and in the way they are dividing their parenting roles. They had known that they eventually wanted children, and Barb had been concerned that, like friends of hers, she might have trouble getting pregnant. Bob was worried about the financial responsibility, and around the time Barb became pregnant, he became much busier in his new medical practice. Barb relied on Bob for answers to medical questions; otherwise, she tended to turn to her girlfriends.

A feeling of things not going as planned pervades this couple's account of pregnancy, birth, and early parenthood: First, Barb became pregnant earlier than had been expected. Then labor began weeks before the due date and was worse than anticipated; Bob kept leaving the room to make phone calls; Barb needed medication and felt guilty because she thought the Lamaze method counseled otherwise; Bob caught the baby at birth, but forceps had been required first; Barb, uncomfortable, pictured a "bloody mess" and wouldn't look.

The baby was jaundiced and treatments for jaundice interrupted nursing. Barb guiltily discontinued breast feeding when it proved painful and unpleasant. The baby reportedly cried unusually much; and the baby's eyes were crossed, making focusing—and bonding—problematic.

Questions

At what point did you make a decision to have a baby?

How long did you try to conceive before you actually did?

From whom and in what activities did you get support during the pregnancy period?

What surprises did you encounter
   during pregnancy?
   during labor?
   during delivery?

How big, how unsettling did the surprises feel to you?

How much did they get in the way of your good feelings
   about yourself
      as a person?
      as a parent?
   about your relationship with your baby's other parent?
   about your baby?

II. Cathy and Curt give the picture of an "evolving" relationship. They were high school sweethearts, but do not seem to have taken their relationship for granted. They seem to know each other well and to feel comfortable with each other. Their readiness to have a baby vacillated for a time between them, first one and then the other expressing the negative side of their ambivalence. They waited until they both felt ready.

Curt says he felt they had both been pregnant. He conscientiously had timed and recorded Cathy's contractions at home for thirty-two hours before they arrived at the hospital and was furious that the staff there gave him no credit for his competence or involvement.

These parents feel that they are both involved in giving care to the baby. In addition, they feel Curt takes care of Cathy, while she takes care of the baby. They seem to be relating to the baby as a developing person and are interested in seeing how relationships evolve within their family.

Questions

Did you and your partner together make the decision to have a baby?

How openly did you address the negative as well as the positive aspects of becoming parents?

Did reactions of medical or paramedical persons disappoint you in some way(s)? How upsetting was this to you?

How much did the surprises you encountered during
pregnancy, labor, and delivery *add* to your good feelings
   about yourself
      as a person?
      as a parent?
   about your baby's other parent
      as a person?
      as a partner?

III. Deirdre and Dan are perhaps most succinctly described as "in love." Each had had one previous marriage. Dan has a handicapped son (age ten) who lives out of state. Dan wanted another child but chose to marry Deirdre knowing she might not want children. With Dan's support, Deirdre sought psychotherapy to help her deal with her fears about having children.

Shortly after they married, they agreed to have a baby on the condition that their relationship with each other remain primary. Their explicit arrangement was that if it didn't work out, they would put the baby up for adoption.

The baby's breech position in the womb required a Caesarean section. Deirdre remained awake; Dan was present. Both were immediately relieved that the baby was healthy and that Deirdre liked the baby at once.

There is a sense that the subjective, "in love" attachment is spreading to include the baby. For instance, when Dan's walking the baby no longer offers her comfort, he passes the baby to Deirdre and continues to sway in rhythm with them for many minutes.

Questions

How helpful, competent, and supportive do you feel medical and paramedical persons were to you?

Were you aware ahead of time of specific concerns you had
   about pregnancy?
   about labor or delivery?
   about the baby?

Did you and your partner each have different concerns? Could you allay each other's worries?

Was there anyone else who could respond supportively and help diminish these worries?

Were these concerns confirmed or allayed by the time your baby was born? Might they linger on awhile?

IV. Erin and Ed are "unconventional"; they are committed to environmental issues. They seem to feel "fate" brought them together, and together they are. They're inseparable, have agreed to always agree, and tend to set themselves apart from others.

Pregnancy was unplanned. It occurred after Erin had separated from her first husband. Erin and Ed made a conscious decision to have Erin secure a divorce, to marry each other, and to keep the baby. They planned a home delivery, but after a labor of three days an infection necessitated going to the hospital. They were both so frightened that upon arrival Ed was doing the Lamaze breathing right along with Erin in order to calm himself as well as to help her.

They found that the hospital experience intruded far less on their exclusive relationship than anticipated. Though sleeping apart from each other felt strange to them, Ed was allowed to visit long hours and could even bring in food from the organic food restaurant they own together.

Now they are dealing with the surprise of how much everything is geared to the baby. They are incorporating her into their "togetherness": The baby sleeps with them, has not been left with anyone else, and they feel no need to leave her.

Questions

Do you think of yourself primarily as part of a couple?

If so, how do you see your baby, and your relationship with your baby, fitting into this sense of yourself?

What changes in your relationship with your partner do you attribute to your having a baby?

Do you feel any need to reserve time for you and your partner to be alone together? If so, are you able to have such time?

V. Fern and Frank have a "modern" marriage. They pursue their own interests. They are open about disagreements and about the importance of their sexual relationship. Fern is a competent executive, and they share financial responsibility for their family. A pregnancy of theirs, which occurred before they were married, had had to be terminated for medical reasons.

Frank sees Fern as having coped well with pregnancy and with the baby, as with everything in general. As a result of Fern's general capability, Frank tended to treat her no differently while she was pregnant; she claims to have wanted him to show more concern. She vetoed his wish for a home delivery, in favor of her doctor's usual practices. She spent the first two hours of labor alone, before waking Frank. They both felt labor was quick and easy. When Frank held the baby in the delivery room, he was so touched that he cried.

They agree that Fern is now the primary caregiver, but Frank makes sure to do at least one care-giving task each day. When Frank holds the baby, the two seem altogether engrossed in each other. Fern plans to return to work soon. Frank would like a clone of himself and of Fern to leave with the baby while they are at work.

Questions

Do you think of yourself primarily as an individual?

If so, how do you see your baby fitting into this sense of yourself?

Have you had to deal with the loss of any relationship that was important to you? Have you come to some sort of peace with this loss so that your energies are free for attaching to your baby?

Do you feel any need to reserve time alone for yourself or time to pursue your own personal career or interests? If so, are you able to have such time?

If the exercise of answering all these questions strikes you as too demanding at first, try to think of it as a diversion from all your daily parenting activities. (The constancy of parenting can get to be a real drag if you allow it to go on completely uninterrupted, you know.)

After you have jotted down or tape recorded your own answers to the above queries, feel quite free to add your own leading questions. Surely this list of questions is not exhaustive. Now that you and your partner have described how you felt about what was happening to and around you—particularly how you felt about yourself, your partner, and your baby—take some time to share your responses with each other.

The next chapter looks more specifically at how your ten new acquaintances are maintaining their balance on the continuum of their lives as they make the transition to parenthood. Perhaps this will prompt you to think further about how you yourself are managing to maintain your own sense of balance during this period.

Knitting Past with Present

Listen as the new parents you met in the last chapter tell you in their own words how it feels to them to be trying to knit together past and present in early parenthood. Like you, they are all trying in their own particular ways to bridge the distance between past and future stages of life.

Erin talks about the difficulties she has had in reconciling her beginning parenthood with images she had of her pre-baby self.

> Those first couple weeks I felt desperately lonely. I felt like I wanted to go back to the restaurant and I felt like I didn't have any . . . I don't know; all of a sudden I felt like my whole previous identity was *erased*, and I was s'pose to be something totally different. . . . I mean I wanted to be her mother and I wanted to mother her; but I didn't want to *not* be that other person. And I was really torn. . . . Well, I decided that I'd have to work on working her into my former identity and working my former identity into her. I'd just have to mesh the whole thing, that's all.

Of course, everyone has a different way of trying to "mesh the whole thing." Your own way will depend on:

—the wishes and obligations you feel you have now as a new parent,

—the particular relationship you have become used to sharing with your partner,

—the anticipating you did (and are doing) about how

your life might go,
—the personal qualities you used to feel were important
parts of *you.*

Surely parenthood does not require that you give up
the qualities that have been important parts of you. As
a matter of fact, parenting your baby capitalizes on one
side of who you used to be. Your new parenthood stirs
up memories of past experiences in which you were in a
caretaker role. Perhaps there were times or situations
when this role was particularly memorable and meaningful to you.

Chances are that as you think about yourself as having
been a caretaker in the past, someone or something will
come to mind as the focus of your earlier caretaking activities and attitudes. Maybe you cared for:

—a younger sibling,
—someone new in your neighborhood,
—a pet,
—some plants,
—a favorite doll.

It might be useful to think about how such past instances
of your caretaking turned out:

—for the object of your care,
—for you, in terms of how you remember feeling at the
    time and what you think and feel when you look back
    now.

Each of your tourmates had some sort of image of having been a caretaker before becoming a parent. Five of
them are members of helping professions. They therefore frequently find themselves in a variety of professional situations that call for their care. These situations
range from those in which these "helping" people feel
effective and gratified to those in which they feel helpless and frustrated. They—and you—need to be able to

come to a self-acceptance in *both* positions.

During those times when your baby seems content, you feel especially effective and gratified in your caregiving role. Your perception of your baby's comfort becomes a barometer you read to indicate that you are handling the current caregiving quite adequately. And if this comfortable equilibrium continues long enough, you may even begin to feel you've got it made!

Then, wham! One day, for some indiscernible reason, your baby is distressed and suddenly seems beyond your ever-increasing repertoire of caregiving, comforting measures. So you feel yourself surprised by a rough push to the helpless-frustrated position. You struggle to keep your balance, to remember that this is certainly far from the whole story. You remind yourself that you really are generally a quite good-enough caregiver. You've proven it in your pre-parenthood past, when you've taken care of other persons or things as well as anyone could have expected.

This is not to suggest that you rest on formerly earned laurels. However, your entire image of yourself as a good-enough caretaker need not depend on a temporary inability to decipher your baby's cues and meet the needs of the very moment. You will be better equipped to communicate to your baby the necessary reassurance, which comes from confidence in yourself as a caretaker, if you can keep in mind: .

—successful instances of earlier caretaking—with your baby or before your baby appeared,
—what you learned as a result of former care-taking experiences.

In short, the caretaker role isn't altogether new. You've been in this spot before.

For example, take the experiences of those other five new acquaintances of yours, those who are not members of helping professions:

Fern spoke of her teenage "babysitting career." So as she tells it, even back then she was meshing her caretaking abilities with her career orientation.

Barb's dog went with her into her marriage. He is cared for so much that both she and Bob wrote "Blackie" when asked to list "others in household."

And Frank responded to Fern's pregnancy by getting a puppy, for whom he considered himself the "primary caretaker." For him, this represented a conscious effort to practice his tolerance of parenthood. He figured if he didn't get "bent out of shape" by the puppy, he'd be okay—patient enough—as a caretaker with the baby as well.

Before they met, Erin and Ed each had tried to help a troubled youngster for some prolonged period of time. Neither of them had found the involvement altogether satisfactory. It had proved none-too-easy to be an effective caretaker. Yet they learned, as perhaps you have also learned:

—how some aspects of caretaking are more difficult than anticipated,
—how real the limitations can be for *anyone* in such circumstances,
—how good it felt, in any case,
  —to have wanted to make the effort,
  —to have given to another person emotionally,
  —to have had the "staying power" to remain available through some rough times,
  —to have grown as a caretaker from the experience.

In addition to the specific perceptions you have of yourself as a present and past caretaker, there are some more general perceptions you have of who you used to be. Some of these perceptions remain constant and may feel consistent with who you are now. Others may feel out of place with your life as it is now. Sorting this out can help you focus on what is constant about you that might lend a balancing hand amid the newness:

—your wishes, goals, values,
—your way of perceiving people and situations,
—your personal style and manner of relating to others.

What qualities—traits, values, interests—do you feel were important parts of who *you* used to be? It is difficult to develop a "stepped back" perspective and to think in specific terms about yourself. Maybe the experiences of your tourmates will trigger some further ideas about just how *you* remain a constant, and how you see yourself as different now that you are a parent.

Erin and Ed see themselves as very "flexible" people. This characteristic is important enough to them that they've taken pride in viewing themselves this way. The ongoing demands of adapting to their baby's needs, schedule, and personality supply ample opportunities for them to prove to themselves over and over again how flexible they still are, how well they can "roll with the punches."

Barb had difficulty meshing her former image of herself as a tidy person with her experience of trying to nurse her baby.

> Yeah, physically (laugh) when I was breast feeding, it was very wet. You're always leaking and everything else. It's just, you don't feel yourself. But now I'm feeling back to normal. . . . Well, the bottle's a lot easier.

It was so important for Barb to regain her sense of continuity with who and how she used to be that she was even willing to pay the price of feeling guilty about her "failure" to breast feed.

Cathy seems to have a sense of both continuity and interruption as she considers how she is now and how she used to be:

> I think I'm just getting adjusted to the role of being a mother. I started to do a little work in the last week . . . and that feels good; so I know I can still be a professional, too. . . . We used to have a pretty active social life. . . . But, like I read the Arts and Fun section every Sunday, and there are all these wonderful things going on that I'm not seeing, so, . . . I miss that kind of thing. So that's one of the drawbacks of parenthood.

Although right now Cathy isn't in a position to do the things she used to do, this interruption will be only temporary. She clearly sees herself as still having some of the same interests she used to have.

Curt pictures himself as the same person he used to be. But now, keeping a hold on his former self, he feels something new has been added—his fatherhood:

> I feel proud, more complete. . . . I'm not only a person and a professional and a friend and all the other things I used to be, but I'm also a father.

The problem is how to fit yet another role, another self-image, into the finite amount of time available each day. Curt is attempting to work out this problem for himself:

> I'm in the process of struggling with compressing alone time. Where I used to go for the whole day to the forest preserves alone, now I have to do that in minutes. . . . But (he brightens noticeably) I've got plans to take her (the baby).

And what about the particular relationship you had grown used to sharing with your partner? How much time are you making to preserve the connections you had going for you with your baby's other parent? This too can offer you an important linkage with your past.

Deirdre almost consciously used her marriage to ease

her transition into parenthood. She and Dan had a con-
tract with each other to maintain the primacy of their
relationship even after the baby's arrival. If you recall,
they had agreed ahead of time that they would not let
anything, even the baby, interrupt their relationship. As
Deirdre put it:

> That was another pleasant surprise, because I al-
> ways anticipated that it would be real difficult and
> uncomfortable and miserable to have sex and we
> probably wouldn't have as much of it—both late in
> pregnancy and soon after childbirth. And that just
> wasn't true for us at all. . . . They said the tradi-
> tional "Resume relations in four to six weeks." But
> we figured that, with a C-section, there's no episi-
> otomy, there's no problem and so after the red blood
> stopped, we resumed. . . . And both of us seemed
> to have the same level of desire and interest as before.

The very act of anticipating how life might be and how
one would like it to be—of mentally projecting yourself
ahead in time—is a kind of preparatory bridging to your
future, another possible way of effectively easing your
transition to parenthood.

Frank found such anticipating helpful immediately after
the baby was born, in dealing with the decrease in sexual
activity, activity that he feels is such an important element in his marriage:

> There's a difference when something's anticipated
> and when it's a surprise. . . . When it's a surprise
> you feel you've lost something that you've had. But
> if you know about it ahead of time . . . it doesn't
> feel the same way, because you're prepared for
> it. . . . I'd read enough to realize that just before
> and after there would be a loss of sexual inter-
> course. . . . Six weeks seemed like a long time. I'd
> heard like certainly three or four. But the fact that I

knew there would be a period when we couldn't have sex afterwards, more or less prepared me. But, you know, I did feel very horny during that period.

The other aspect of future orientation that may help you "mesh the whole thing" is your sense of belonging to a kind of Parental Community. This was even a prime motivating factor in Barb and Bob's deciding just when to have a baby: "All our friends were starting to have families." Their own circle of long-time friends could serve as a ready-made support group and link with their past as non-parents and with their future as parents.

But perhaps Curt put the feeling of membership in the Parental Community most graphically:

> As soon as you're with another couple who has a baby, you're immediately connected by virtue of the fact that you're in the same cult. It doesn't matter where, what you do for a living, or who you are. I mean, you can talk about how you fold the diapers, how-what-where she sleeps, how you stick her foot in her pajamas—anything! . . . People who don't have babies are not interested in what you're interested in. They don't care about whether snaps are better than buttons on terry suits. And frankly, I can't imagine that I'm talkin' about it either! But, man, it's fine!

To Curt it seems unnecessary to coordinate parenthood with friends' timing of this event, as Barb and Bob did. Rather, he feels that you need only be open to sharing your experiences with other new parents and you are bound to come up with your own local chapter of the Parental Community.

Even Erin and Ed, who tend to set themselves apart from others, seem to be experiencing a wish to be part of the Parental Community. Ed's account points to a shift in their willingness to affiliate with other new parents since their baby was born:

> The last week we were in Lamaze class, this woman came in from this group called Mothers' Helpers and she just wanted us to know that they were there when we had questions. And she passed around cards so she could get our names and numbers. And we just took one look at her and we took one look at each other, and we said, "Thanks, we'll pass." . . . We're kind of skeptical of other people in a lot of ways. I mean, we really have our own ideas, you know; we like to develop our own ideas. . . . There are people like us, like we know now all of a sudden three or four couples who have babies or just had babies and we're all gonna get together. . . . We feel like we can exchange stories and learn things from them, you know what I mean.

So how is it going for you, this holding on to the past *you* and anticipating the future *you*? Why not call up some member(s) of your local chapter of the Parental Community and swap stories of how you're doing with this knitting together of your past and present images of yourselves? Then you can return to the next chapters to consider the historical events you experienced en route to parenthood.

The Push Into Parenthood

In the last chapter, you considered how some parts of *you*, Pre-Baby, have accompanied the Post-Baby *you*. Perhaps you thought of some additional ways to knit together your past images of yourself with your present images. Now, to gain further balance, please accompany the tourmates you recently met on a guided journey into your past. In this chapter you'll visit the most nearby historical sites on your road to parenthood—your labor and delivery.

You probably have some vivid impressions or definite feelings about the circumstances and events of your own labor and delivery. What were these happenings like for you? Did you have:

—a planned Caesarean section, a relatively quick operation, like the one Deirdre and Dan felt was so easy?

—a medically-induced labor like Barb's (prescribed because her water bag broke and labor failed to start), or like Cathy's (prescribed to speed up a thirty-two-hour labor)?

—an efficient six-hour labor, which Fern found surprisingly speedy?

—an "endless" labor of three days, which Erin and Ed went through?

Labor-and-delivery was the most immediate precursor to your parenthood, highlighting your scene with vivid colors:

—red, for angry or hurt or ashamed,
—yellow, for warm and satisfied,

—green, for new and unripe, and maybe not quite ready
for what's coming,
—blue, for disappointed, sad at losing something,
—purple, for proud that you did it, that your baby deigned
to dub thee "parent."   -

Because this experience was so significant for you, the
feelings it stimulated tend to be lasting ones. So the rainbow of feelings you experienced at that time arches over
from labor-and-delivery into your present, coloring how
you see things and respond to them today.

Perhaps, like your tourmates, you took a "natural"
childbirth class to prepare yourself for labor and delivery. Perhaps you, like they, found such classes useful.
Your new acquaintances felt the classes had taught them
what was to be expected within the realm of "normal"
occurrences in labor and delivery.

The one reservation often expressed about such classes
is the feeling of guilt that people tend to have when—
for whatever reason—it turns out that they were not
able to go through with as much of the "natural" childbirth program as they had wanted and intended. These
guilt feelings are unfortunate because they run counter
to the very purpose of these programs: to minimize the
anxieties of expectant parents by familiarizing the parents with the whole range of possible courses labor and
delivery might take, thus enabling them to cope more
easily with whatever occurs. If guilt feelings creep in,
they are probably due more to individuals' personal
wishes—their own mindset, which prompted involvement in the classes in the first place—than to explicit
messages given by teachers of these classes. In any case,
this guilt can turn out to be an additional burden for new
parents—all of whom have quite enough to deal with
already, as you can attest.

Of course, it would be understandable to feel *disappointed* if something you thought important didn't go as

you had planned. You might feel disappointed in your own lack of preparation, in your doctor, or even in your own or your partner's body for not complying with your expectations. But guilt, and the self-blame that goes with it, is uncalled for, not constructive, and potentially disruptive. That is not to say that you ought to feel guilty about feeling guilty, for heaven's sake! Rather, it would be more productive for you:

—to allow yourself to feel sad at the disappointment,
—to come to terms with the notion that you couldn't have controlled the particular turn events took,
—to go on, guiltlessly.

It would be truly unfortunate if feelings that you somehow "should have done it differently" were to get in the way of your parenting. Surely you are not a lesser parent if you couldn't follow through on your "natural" childbirth plan, or feel in as much control of the situation as you'd hoped, or be quick enough getting to the hospital and the anesthetist's help to prevent all that pain, or even if you couldn't respond immediately with all the wonderful parental emotions you expected to experience.

Once again, it might be helpful for you to jot down or tape record what you remember feeling at the time, and what you feel now in retrospect about your labor and delivery experiences. You may then find it easier to uncover similar patterns of feelings as you move along on this guided tour of your past. If you can discern your typical patterns, you can begin to see that the ways in which you perceive your new parenthood and respond to your baby and your partner fit rather neatly on the continuum of your life.

Reviewing the historical events of your immediate past is a means of gaining perspective, of putting these past events more or less to rest. Then the disappointments, hurts, and anger you may have experienced at the time will be less apt to disrupt such crucial current developments as:

—your attachment to your baby,
—your view of yourself as a parent,
—your view of your partner as a parent,
—your relationship with your partner.

Whatever feelings may linger on about your labor and delivery, they were relatively compact experiences, a matter of hours or at most a few days in duration. The next historical event on your tour into your immediate past, the pregnancy period, covers a bit more time. It may well seem upstaged by the more recent experience of labor and delivery—and by your baby, that not-all-glittering pot of gold you met on this end of the rainbow.

Whether you consider labor and delivery to have been hard or easy, you may see these as unusual, isolated events in your history. The way you remember feeling and behaving during that time may seem unlikely to represent patterns typical of you.

By comparison, pregnancy was longer and gave you more time to develop attitudes, try out different ways of dealing with the experience as it unfolded. Whether you feel your pregnancy was hard or easy, it could not have flashed by without affecting you in some ways, without evoking responses in you. After all, you coped, you made it through.

Being an extended period, pregnancy parallels the longer transitional period you are now passing through—beginning parenthood. How you responded to the earlier transition of pregnancy is likely to be repeated in how you respond to your current transitional situation. It may prove useful to you, therefore, to focus on how pregnancy affected you and which of your methods of dealing with this experience were helpful and which were not. This exploration might offer you a perspective on what methods of coping:

—are typical of you,
—might be useful to you now in early parenthood,
—might be worth your attempting to alter in some way,
—might be missing from your repertoire that others have found work well for them.

The next chapter invites you to continue your tour to gain this "pregnant perspective."

Growing While You Wait

Your tour of the pregnancy period covers more time than did last chapter's review of labor and delivery. A planned itinerary may make this chapter's visits more manageable. So plan first to get an overview of your pregnancy experience—a general impression—and then later to examine certain sections of it in greater detail. What comes to mind first when you think about your pregnancy as a total experience? You may want to take a few moments to think and to jot down your thoughts and feelings before reading on to compare notes with your new acquaintances.

An Overview of Pregnancy

Barb and Bob focused first on how Barb had felt sick and how important it had been for her to have the support of friends who had just gone through the same stages. As Bob explained,

> Two of our friends were pregnant before Barb, so you know, the first one was on her own; the second one has the first one; then Barb has both of them. You know, "What does it feel like?" And this and that.

By contrast, Erin's initial response to the question of how pregnancy went for her was "Real well, I was real healthy." While Barb and Bob had continued their pattern of supportive relationships with friends, Erin and Ed had found support in their continuing togetherness with each other, doing everything together, including their pattern of eating organic food, which for them symbolized their restaurant, their lifestyle, their togetherness. Ed talked about how their friends expected them to produce "The Organic Kid." Erin àgreed, quoting a typical conversation,

> "Well, this is gonna be a healthy baby, right?" "Well, I guess so, I mean I hope so! If she's not, boy! We're really in trouble." You eat organic food and you eat vegetarian and, you know, this is gonna have to be really a healthy baby. And . . . I did feel *pressure* for her to be healthy: I felt a lot of pressure!

Fern and Frank had also continued their earlier relationship pattern—doing their own things. They felt basically that pregnancy had not changed their lives much. Fern's initial response was that she "remained extremely active and still doing things." And Frank reflected,

> I probably didn't treat Fern much differently during her pregnancy than before. . . . I was always ready to do things like lifting things and making sure that I would carry heavy things and so forth because I would be aware that that would be a strain on her. But outside of that I don't know that I treated her too much differently. . . . One thing was that she had a pretty easy pregnancy . . . so outside of the fact that she was bulging in the front and getting bigger, there wasn't that much, not so many other things that were involved.

This contrasted with Cathy's description of how Curt responded to her being pregnant:

> It brought out all of his nurturing qualities. I mean, he took such good care of me. . . . Of course, I felt more justified being more dependent. But he also was wonderful, you know (laugh). I'd be lying in

bed at night and say, "Oh, I would just love an orange." And he'd go downstairs and bring me up an orange. I mean, he was just so nurturing and caring, it was just wonderful.

And Curt proudly confirmed her report: "It's true, it's all true."

So whether you feel that you did your own separate coping with pregnancy, or that you tended to get support directly from your partner, or from your relationship with your partner or others (friends, relatives, medical personnel, authors), chances are that this is your typical way of perceiving and handling your life. You didn't just invent this out of the blue as a way to deal with pregnancy. (The chapter "Once Upon Your Moms and Dads" will further explore this background.) It most likely was a way that you had found useful for both you and your partner even before this pregnancy occurred. In any case, because it is so familiar to you, it probably helped ease your transition into and throughout pregnancy. And your own typical ways of perceiving and handling happenings are still available to you; they are (or could be) operating for you now, in early parenthood.

Perhaps, though, you think that your typical ways of perceiving and handling happenings in the past left something to be desired. Then possibly the experience of one or more of your new acquaintances could suggest additional (or alternative) ways that you may want to try out in dealing with happenings now. The purpose here is not to stir up regrets about your past, but rather to learn from it—and maybe from the experiences of others as well—so that the going will be as smooth as possible now and tomorrow for you, your partner, and your baby.

Now, as you review your pregnancy, you can organize your recollections in several ways. First, you can view your experience in units of time, looking at the nine months in smaller segments. Then you can view it by recalling how you functioned—your means of communication, your choice of medical support, your eating and sleeping arrangements, your experiences of body changes.

A View of Your Pregnancy by Time Segments

To begin, try to look at your pregnancy in smaller units of time. You already may have broken up the nine months in your mind according to whatever major shifts you think occurred over the pregnancy period. Did you undergo any emotional changes during the nine months—shifts in feelings about yourself, about your status of Parent-To-Be, your uppermost concerns and pleasures? You may already have mentally divided pregnancy according to your own particular sense of just when, at what points, you experienced changes.

Perhaps you lump together the first eight months and then separate out the ninth month as different. Take Erin's account, for example:

> I worked right up to the last month, when I was just really heavy and kinda sluggish and . . . it was hot and I really wasn't . . . that good. People just bumped into me a lot, so I sorta got outa the way. . . . I stayed home and got things ready.

Or perhaps you think in terms of the first and second halves of this experience, like Fern and Frank do.

Frank: I think that in the early part of Fern's pregnancy, she was very, very concerned that she'd miscarry. She had thought that she would have trouble getting pregnant; and she thought that she might have trouble carrying her pregnancy to term; she was worried about . . . a spontaneous abortion.

Fern: But after I got beyond that point, I was no longer

concerned that it was going to abort at midpoint . . . and I was feeling fairly good, and because of that I assumed that everything was fine.

Yet Fern reported that she had experienced mood swings
from the midpoint of her pregnancy on.

I'm normally a fairly "up" person to begin with,
and so . . . I'm normally feeling really good. But the
swings down I did notice because I realized they
weren't *me*.

Fern went on immediately, automatically trying to make
these swings down fit in with her earlier experience of
herself, so they would not have to remain so uncomfortably unfamiliar to her.

I connected them with mood swings I frequently
got with my periods before I was pregnant. I would
either start crying very easily or get very angry and
start yelling a lot.

Or perhaps, like Cathy and Curt, you tend to think of
the pregnancy period in terms of its trimesters. After
describing the overall experience of pregnancy as "wonderful," Cathy broke it down as follows:

The first three months were really hard. . . . I wasn't
as sick as a lot of women are, but for me, I hate
being nauseous, and I was fairly nauseous. I didn't
really throw up much at all, but . . . I think I was
real scared and felt very vulnerable and very dependent. And I was, you know, really afraid whether I
could do this thing, have a baby. I think partly the
physiological thing, going through a pregnancy—
would it be okay?—going through labor; and then
also being a parent. I wanted it but I was also scared.
I was . . . feeling very vulnerable and needy during that first trimester, so that was kinda hard. And
also I wasn't feeling very good, so it wasn't like this

joyous, wonderful thing. But from the second trimester on, I really enjoyed it a lot. I felt good, and I felt like I looked good, and I liked the way my body looked, and I was much more excited; I wasn't so scared. I guess I had my moments, probably, of being afraid; but I really enjoyed it. . . . I mean, I think toward the end, I was . . . more scared about labor than about being a parent.

Curt, too, after describing his general feeling about this nine-month period, divided the pregnancy into trimesters, giving a clear picture of how his feelings shifted through this time.

(Laugh) It was surreal. It was really surreal, because it was hard to believe; it took a long time to believe. The first trimester was trying because she wasn't feeling well; the second trimester was euphoric, 'cause she was really ridin' high; and the third trimester was let's-get-this-friggin'-thing-over-with-already, because, you know, you're ready for it by that time. Yeah, at the beginning of the third trimester, right. I was ready. I was tired of being pregnant already. . . . I did feel like *we* were pregnant, in a sense.

People seem mentally to divide time periods into smaller units rather automatically, possibly without being aware that they do so. Although the divisions vary from person to person (or at least from couple to couple), the fact that the dividing occurs with a degree of frequency suggests that it has some purpose(s). Perhaps dividing up a long span of time serves to organize the experiences in one's mind, allowing them to become more comprehensible. Perhaps, too, such divisions serve as welcome markers of how far one has progressed, how many milestones one's been able to pass (if not to whiz right by) in transit.

So now in the transition of early parenthood, you may

find yourself mentally dividing this period into smaller units of time:

—the days in the hospital, the days with extra help at home, the weeks of parenting pretty much on your own;

—"day" and "night" are differentiated in your mind, even though your parenting activities may actually make the distinction a bit blurry;

—your baby is a week or two weeks or a whole month old, and it seems so momentous an occasion that you feel like staging a major celebration;

—appointments with your pediatrician get counted by you serially, or by the number of immunizations your baby has received.

Such dividing may prove useful. You are attempting, after all, to build order back into your life, to organize events in your mind so that you can grasp what's happened and cope with what comes next. The milestones you pass, however close together they may be placed, give you a more definite reading on how far you've managed to get and convince you that you are indeed making some headway, no matter how endless the path may seem.

A View of Your Pregnancy by Tasks

Besides dividing up pregnancy in smaller, more easily grasped units of time, you can also look at pregnancy in terms of tasks you had to accomplish. For example, consider the tasks of your *communications department*. Perhaps you shared Curt's attitude that you and your partner were a pregnant couple, going through the experience together. Or maybe you felt more alone as you experienced this pregnancy. Whatever your attitude, it was shaped by and reflected in the particular means of communication you and your partner used with each other and with others during the pregnancy period. For one example of your communication style, consider first how you handled the official report that you had conceived a baby. Perhaps you greeted the news with shock or surprise, relief or excitement, concern or worry. In any case, there were the decisions about whom to tell:

—your parents, relatives,
—your friends, neighbors,
—your employer(s), co-workers,

and when to tell them:

—maybe the news felt too exciting for you to wait an extra minute;
—maybe you felt you'd better wait until later in the pregnancy, when chances of miscarriage were less;
—maybe there were certain people whom you wanted to tell first, and since they happened to be away on vacation when you got The Word, you chose to hold on to your news until they got home;

and how to tell them:

—you dropped choice hints;
—you arranged a special time for folks to get together with you both so you could make the Big Announcement;
—you picked up the phone and together called people, or each independently told your own friends and relatives;
—you waited for people to notice and ask.

Your particular way of handling the news could tell you a lot about your levels of enthusiasm, anxiety, mutual participation with your partner, and interest in sharing the experience with others.

The benefit of hindsight in observing your feelings and behaviors in the face of your Big News can help you become more aware of your patterns and allow you to better understand and monitor your present situation and current reactions. Do you tend to:

—look forward to new situations and feel some confidence that you'll be able to handle them well enough?
—approach newness with enough eagerness (and, yes, anxiety) to be motivated and ready to take on what comes?
—reach the point of feeling so overwhelmed that you are even anxious about being anxious?
—get from others just about the responses you either wanted or expected?
—not give much of a hoot about how others respond, because it truly doesn't matter to you, or because you've felt too disappointed by others in the past?
—set yourself up for disappointment by being so off-hand or indirect that others can't know what's important to you, or by building your expectations so high that no reality could live up to them?
—"tell it like it is," so others can understand how you feel?

It is possible for you to monitor your responses and purposely alter certain of your patterns in ways you think may help you to deal better with your current situation. (You will come to some examples of such monitoring in the chapter "Once Upon Your Moms and Dads.") You are not aiming for any deep personality change but for a plan of coping and communicating that may make life (and early parenthood) a bit easier and more gratifying for you. (See the chapter "Who Cares About Parents, Anyway?" for further tips on altering communication patterns.)

Now, moving along on your tour of pregnancy, please direct your attention to the *medical department*. In this area first you arranged for the medical services you wanted to have available to you for pre-natal care; then you responded to the services as they were provided. Obstetric visits were an important activity during pregnancy. They served to:

—divide pregnancy into expectably shorter and shorter lengths of time between appointments, marking your headway in approaching the birthing goal;
—give you the sense that you had something definite to do for your baby (keep regular appointments);
—provide some way of checking on your baby's progress;
—supply some general directives to serve as a kind of health insurance;
—offer some expert reassurances about developments of baby and mother-to-be;
—relieve you and your partner of having to carry the entire responsibility of monitoring the pregnancy, allowing you to share it appropriately with a medical specialist;
—convey the comfort that someone out there cares, and that you, your health, and your baby's health are to be taken seriously as matters worthy of concern.

Pediatric visits are serving similar purposes for you now during early parenthood. How you are responding now to your baby's pediatric care may be in some way(s) similar to your earlier responses in the medical department. Again, it might be helpful to look for your patterns.

At times you may play nip and tuck with going to the pediatrician for regular appointments. The weather may be so bad it seems unwise to take your baby out; or your baby doesn't seem quite up to par today and you feel you shouldn't aggravate the situation further with an exam or inoculation; or you've heard there's a lot of flu going around now, and you wouldn't want your baby in the doctor's waiting room where exposure to this—or worse!—seems likely. (It's hard to be convinced that your baby is still likely to be protected by Mom's antibodies.) You battle it out in private dialogue in your mind, or perhaps your partner or doctor obligingly takes the opposite side of the debate.

Do you recall having any such debates during pregnancy with regard to visits to the obstetrician? Before answering no, think about whether you ever thought or talked with your partner about postponing an appointment because the weather was wet or icy (or hot and sticky) and slipping and falling (or heat exhaustion) seemed a risk to be avoided; or because the mom-to-be wasn't feeling up to par and might feel all the more touchy or tired if she were to trek all the way to the doctor and be examined; or because you were concerned that lately the mom-to-be had not been eating at all according to the diet your doctor had prescribed, and you wanted a little extra time to see if the scale might register a better balance. If you postponed obstetric appointments, or often considered doing so during pregnancy, and find yourself nowadays tending to stretch out the amount of time between pediatric visits, you may just be looking for good excuses. You might ask yourself what needs you may have that are being served by these delaying tactics. Could it be that you typically become:

—leery that you might disagree with some suggestions your doctor might make and want to avoid confrontations?

—frustrated, feeling that appointments seem like they will be taking up so much of your time forever, and wondering whether the directives provided are worth all the bother?

—anxious about giving up much responsibility for your baby to anyone else, even a medical person?

—uneasy that your doctor will be patronizing (or not solicitous enough), stirring up dependency wishes that you might find confusing?

—worried that your doctor will be overtly or silently critical of you in your new role, stirring up feelings of shame or guilt that you might find unsettling?

Or perhaps you found that checkups were spaced too far apart for you, that you preferred to check in more frequently. And if you feel that your visits with your pediatrician similarly are too far apart, do you think you have become:

—concerned that your doctor will not be able to learn who you are, the way you personally want things to go with your baby?
—embarrassed that you may fail to make enough of an impression, so that your doctor may be unable to remember your name, or your baby's name, or the details of your situation?
—upset, thinking some vague thing might have gone amiss between regular visits?
—distressed or guilty, knowing that you or your partner disregarded some doctor's order, and fearing this may have brought some harm to your baby?

Whether you find yourself or your partner tending to alter the spacing of checkups, or whether you make and keep appointments on the prescribed schedule, it may be useful to have a clear idea of the various uses these contacts have for you, as well as for your baby. They can help:

—provide you with some rather concrete directives,
—measure your baby's progress,
—reassure you in the face of some worries and fears you may have,
—relieve you of having medical responsibilities heaped upon all the other parental responsibilities you have,
—give you a sense that someone else cares, lending professional weight to your own conviction that your baby's health, your baby, and you all count.

You are entitled to all of the above. But at times, of course, you may feel somewhat disappointed by what your doctor offers—he, too, being human and able to supply only "good-enough" and not perfect care. However, if you are clear about what your medical care can provide, you might then be in a position to:

—combat the vague sense that something is unsatisfactory,
—pinpoint what more you need,
—discuss your need directly with your doctor so that you might satisfactorily resolve your feeling of disappointment,
—go on making use of what services *are* being offered.

Now proceed on your tour with a look at the *body care department* of your pregnancy. Body care tasks involve patterns of eating and exercise, patterns of dealing with physical symptoms and experiences of body changes, and patterns of sexual interacting. Each of these areas probably required you to make some adjustments during pregnancy, so they can be used to give you some feedback about how you reacted to that particular time of transition—and hence some clues about how you are reacting in this new transitional time, early parenting.

Possibly, at some point in your pregnancy—with or without your doctor's advice—you and your partner together made some change in dietary or exercise habits. This change could have brought about some weight gain or loss for the expectant father as well as for the mother-to-be. Weight gain in an expectant father might indicate a wish to participate in the growing and nurturing of the baby or a feeling that he is, will be, taking on quite a lot. On the other hand, the weight loss in a father-to-be might point to a wish to be fit, ready, in shape for what's coming. Or it could represent an attempt to compensate for his partner's weight gains and an effort to keep things on an even keel. Or maybe weight loss signals a worry that this beginning of parenthood might be something of a drain.

Moreover, during this period whatever physical symptoms appeared in either expectant partner—tiredness, vomiting, nightmares, anxiety—just might have expressed an emotional as well as a physical reaction to the transition into parenthood. Underlying emotional reactions that erupt as physical symptoms have to be dealt with. Of course, whatever symptoms you may have had were *real* and had to be treated accordingly. (Indeed, whatever "morning sickness" may express in terms of an emotional transition, nausea is still nausea. And the nearness of a friendly local bathroom is still important.) But symptoms may also have been signposts that marked outlets for feelings. They may indicate that the emotional transition was more difficult than you were aware of. Some physical symptoms may even serve as a kind of rite of passage, a formal ritual that officially ushers in a new life phase.

It is as if the new life phase of parenthood—membership in the parental fraternity—has a nine-month pledge period. The magnitude of the change taking place may call for more fanfare than is offered by simply and gradually looking increasingly pregnant. More obvious signs (other physical symptoms) may serve—rather like the tasks assigned to those pledging a fraternity—to bring home the reality that the new phase is approaching and that the parents-to-be are in process of earning full membership in the parental fraternity. Such obvious signs may be particularly useful in early pregnancy for the mother-to-be, and in later pregnancy for the participating father-to-be. At these times physical symptoms can counteract the rather vague sense that change is coming and offer something more definite to experience.

To some parents-to-be the unknown changes of the pregnancy period loom so frighteningly in their future that they try to postpone them as long as possible. They may resist accommodating their schedules to new requirements for resting or eating, or they may conceal or deny the telling signs when the pregnancy begins to show. Many parents-to-be worry that the with-child body (one's own or one's partner's) will be less attractive to them, aesthetically or sexually, than that same body was, pre-pregnancy. Getting used to a whole different contour in one's own body, or even in a partner's, does not happen immediately or automatically. Here, too, it takes time to gain comfort, to accustom oneself.

Did you give yourself the necessary time and allow yourself your partner's support—such as reassurances about your continued attractiveness to him or her; about your feeling that your attraction to him or her will resume along with the pre-baby contours; about the efficiency and elegance of reproductory equipment, male and female? As you consider what was your own process of acclimating to the pregnant body in your midst, typical patterns may again emerge:

—inclinations to deny difficulties even to yourself (strivings to keep your former balance, despite incompatible changes in what used to be your status quo);

—tendencies to handle things independently of your partner (wishes to see yourself or your partner or both of you as totally competent and self-assured);

—hesitancies to communicate about sensitive issues important to you (efforts to hide your feelings of vulnerability);

—preferences to participate together in various aspects of this new experience (desires to work out a comfortable, mutual dependency).

Which of these patterns do you think served you well during pregnancy? This is important to consider because you want your new baby to become comfortable with his or her own growing body. You and your partner can contribute to your baby's sense of body comfort if you are able to acclimate and re-acclimate to the body changes your baby will undergo and if you can convey comfortably positive feelings about your own bodies.

Chances are, the ease or difficulty you had in accepting body changes during pregnancy echoed earlier reactions you had, say, to adolescent changes in your body and in your developing awareness of your sexuality. The point is that your attitudes about sexuality—including perceptions of your body and your partner's body, of your sexual capacities and vulnerabilities and those of your partner—predate this pregnancy. So your feelings and responses during this nine-month period cannot in fairness be pinned on your baby. Your pregnancy did not feel as it did because your baby-to-be had certain personality traits already genetically in the making. Recognizing this could help free you from a tendency to make assumptions about what this baby will be like, based on how you perceive your pregnancy—difficult or easy, tiring or stimulating, dependable or unpredictable.

The temptation to jump to conclusions about your baby during pregnancy (and even at this stage of early parenthood) is great since you are indeed incredibly curious to know more than you possibly can about your child-to-be. Again, you run the risk of creating expectations for your baby to live up to, fall short of, or just get lost in. Whatever the outcome, the expectations are a heavy lot to heap upon so small a person. Yet, just waiting around, containing all your curiosity and refraining from making any predictions about the small person who is developing, can make for a very slow nine-month passage.

Some expectant couples resist a passive waiting for the gradual changes of pregnancy. They need to feel more active in coping with what is happening to them, to their lives. This was so for each of the couples accompanying you on your tour. They each chose to make other external changes in their lives during the pregnancy period—

moves to a new house or job—changes they viewed as "significant life events." Did you decide to make such changes in your life while pregnancy was in progress?

Rationally, one might expect people to avoid making further changes at such a time, heaping change upon change. But perhaps these external changes serve as happenings that people can more readily control and manage than the pregnancy itself or traits of the baby-to-be. Surely one could hope to have more of a sense of mastery in making a transition to a new home or a different job situation than in making the more amorphous transition into parenthood.

So if you managed some concrete, external change during pregnancy, perhaps you approach early parenthood with proof that you *can* cope. It can only help to have such reassurance, to feel that you are able to regain a balance in your life.

And if you did not happen to make external changes in your life during pregnancy, well, obviously, you made it through without doing so. You may have felt quite okay, and that's great! By all means follow the old adage: "If it works, don't fix it!" Then again, you may have felt off-balance even though you did make it through pregnancy. Now, however, managing the more concrete tasks of parenting may help you feel more active in coping with your current situation. It might be reassuring to recognize how different it feels to have more definite things to do—feeding, cleaning, holding—than the nine months of waiting offered you.

Should these concrete tasks of parenting not prove especially reassuring, it might be useful now to take on a manageable project with both a clear beginning and a clear end—one in which you can see yourself making definite progress—whether it be a potluck get-together with friends or reading the next chapter of this book. Making an opportunity to demonstrate to yourself your effectiveness as a person can only add to your sense of adequacy as a parent.

Continuing your tour of the *baby care department* of your pregnancy, consider your sexual interaction activity, which was probably disturbed by pregnancy. Your sexual functioning is important to think about because it is both an aspect of your self and part of your relationship with your partner. Your sexual functioning is also important because it is both a past fact and a future option, even if it is not currently much of a viable possibility. In spanning your past and your future, your sexual functioning can offer you and your partner a sense of stability as you go through the none-too-settling present.

But what, if any, directive did your doctor give you about your sexual relationship during pregnancy? Was this subject brought up or avoided by either of you? Was your experience anything like what Frank and Fern described?

Frank: When Fern got more than three or four months pregnant, I think the amount of times we had sexual activity went down, and of course we had to make some changes in terms of position as she was getting bigger and bigger. But I don't think that it really got me going crazy, I don't think it did that. I would joke about it a lot at work, and of course people would joke about it with me—you know, they'd ask me, "Have you been cut off yet?" you know, and . . . I'd have a lot of fun with that, 'cause I like to joke anyway. . . . But I don't think I was tremendously put out by it.

Fern: Our sexual activity did substantially reduce, and, very honestly, it was because I, for some reason—and I don't know whether it was a hormonal thing or what—I really lost my sexual desire. And it really did not come back till after the baby was born. . . .

Were you as prepared for such a happening ahead of time as they were? Or were you perhaps left to take it personally, as if something must be wrong with you or with your relationship if you or your partner seems to have lost interest sexually? Deirdre and Dan were prepared for this happening, but they had a different experience.

> We had a good sex life up to, oh, two weeks before. . . . It was only after we found out that I was dilating that we stopped . . . (and then only because the mucous plug was out and we were afraid of infection.) . . . I think a continuing interest in sex is unusual because I wasn't experiencing what others in my Lamaze group were talking about . . . but I didn't want to tell people.

Deirdre was afraid others might react with a horrified "Whaaaat?!" The point is that there is no single "right" way. Feelings are simply feelings, and yours are more meaningful and valid *for you* than anyone else's could be.

Some words of caution, however. If you and/or your partner felt uncomfortable relating to each other sexually before your baby was born (or even conceived), there may be a tendency to prolong the postpartum ban on sexual interaction. This can show up as a prolonged concern for the new mother's physical condition. Or maybe you allow your baby to sleep in your bed as an understood prophylactic measure. It might be far more useful to discuss your sexual discomforts directly—with your partner, with your doctor, and/or with another appropriate professional. (See the chapter "Who Cares About Parents, Anyway?")

Or perhaps you were comfortable relating sexually prebaby. But maybe you're being influenced by the old myth that women can be sexy only until they become mothers. After that, they are to be considered "maternal" if not "matronly." You need only look at the advertisements in magazines and on television to see how prevalent this myth is and how it is being perpetuated. It is altogether possible that you and/or your partner—unknowingly having bought into this myth—have some resistance to seeing your own baby's mother regain her former attitudes about herself as a sexual person, someone with sexual needs.

Now, if both you and your partner chance to have the same level of sexual desire postpartum, all's fine. But how often do you suppose that happens? And when that is not the case, the prolonged ban leaves one of you frustrated and potentially resentful. Unfortunately, such resentment easily spreads to your baby to interrupt good feelings about this new person in your midst. This possibility warrants monitoring by you. (You can turn to the last two chapters in this Parents' Needs section for suggestions on monitoring.)

As you conclude this review of your pregnancy period, make a note to give some thought, from time to time, to whatever patterns of feeling and behaving you have discovered. These patterns of yours did not occur by chance and are not likely to remain behind as historical curiosities. You'll want to try to make sure that those patterns you take along with you into parenthood are the ones that serve you well. So you do what you can to discard excess baggage that could slow your progress, and to make full use of patterns that were helpful to you in the past. Other relevant patterns may come to light in the next chapter as you tour the last historical site of your immediate past—your decision to have a baby.

So You Wanted to Be Parents!

Time was when Marriage, the decision of whom to wed, was the Giant Step, because it carried with it the assumption that this was the start of a new family. The first pregnancy usually followed soon after a couple's marriage—or people began to assume that something was amiss. Today, however, marriage itself is not so giant a step. It is more generally acceptable for couples to try living together before deciding to marry. And with modern methods of birth control and increased emphasis on personal freedoms for individuals in a marital relationship, getting married doesn't necessarily imply so big a change. Having children is no longer a silent promise, given and accepted along with the love-honor-and-cherish vows. Having a first baby is a choice. It requires a decision, and it promises much change. It now is the Giant Step.

Can you still recall why you wanted to have a baby, to be a parent? How were you feeling about yourself and about your partner at the time? What prompted you to take the Giant Step at this point in your life and in your relationship with your partner?

Probably when you decided to have a baby, you felt good-enough about yourself already. Neither your status as a parent nor any baby or child of yours can take the place of or compensate for other areas in which you might feel personally and acutely dissatisfied. Oh, having a baby could justify why you must postpone traveling, or changing jobs, or returning to school. But if such activities carry great significance for you in how you view yourself, then having a baby cannot be expected, once and for all, to take care of your personal dreams and anxieties. Your baby cannot be expected to ensure your basic satisfaction with yourself as a man or woman, as a complete person.

There's a catch here: On the one hand you can't expect your baby to take care of your feeling incomplete yourself. Yet, on the other hand, if you didn't feel that life without parenthood might be incomplete, that you'd be missing out on something, why would you have wanted a baby at all?

Like Bob and Barb, had you always known you'd want to have a family and it was simply a matter of timing? Or, like the other four couples, did you actively have to decide not only *when* but *if*, as well? Deirdre, Erin, and Fern all are in second marriages, having chosen not to have babies in their former relationships. They serve as reminders that the opposite decision is indeed a possible alternative.

There are many reasons why you may have made the decision you did. If you were feeling generally worthwhile as a person, good about yourself and your partner, you may have wanted:

—to broaden your roles and your life experiences;
—to express your good feelings in love and care for a child—an extension of yourself, your partner, and your relationship;
—to expand your horizons into the future, your baby offering you a kind of mini-express to immortality;
—to prove that your body was old enough or young enough or in good-enough health to function with its full sexual potential;
—to counteract a feeling that time was running out on your being either:
    —likely to produce a "normal," healthy baby (knowing your chances are better, statistically, if the mother-to-be is under thirty-five years of age), or

—active or patient enough to enjoy, grow with, and
tolerate a child;
—to confirm for yourself, your partner, and/or others
that your life is indeed going along just as you want it
to.

You may have felt basically good about yourself, your
partner, and your situation. Yet as you made your decision to have a baby, you and your partner may have
wondered or worried about whether you would be able
to keep on feeling good about yourselves and each other
in the face of becoming parents. You may have asked
yourselves some general but pointed questions:

—How much time and energy and stimulation and
physical care and love will a baby require of me?
—How much will I be able to give?
—Do I feel strong enough, in good-enough health myself to be able to provide what my baby needs without
becoming depleted and overwhelmed?

No matter how you dealt with such questions in anticipation, they tend to crop up again and again, threatening your sense of adequacy as a parent and a person.
In particular, they come back to mind whenever you are
disappointed in a secret expectation that was important
enough to you to be hidden among your reasons for having a baby in the first place. And in the face of such a
disappointment it might be harder to feel adequate as a
parent. Self-doubt can interrupt your good-enough parenting. So it is important to unmask the ongoing expectations that were part of your decision to have a baby, as
well as the more immediate ones you sniffed out in the
chapter "Dreams Versus Diapers."

One expectation you may have had is that your baby's
personality would be rather like yours, at least basically
compatible with yours. This expectation is not totally
unreasonable; most often babies arrive with character

traits that strike responsive chords in their parents. But you can be seriously disappointed if your baby happened to come with a different temperament than you'd ever bargained for—namely, one quite at odds with yours: Maybe you prefer to be quiet; you drew a baby who seems in perpetual motion. Or maybe you are a "doer" and like to be constantly on the go, while your baby happens to be one who needs an unusual amount of sleep. Or you love to cook and feed others, but your baby is uninterested in eating at times or seems to spit up a lot. Or you tend to accept the world and your place in it on faith, and your baby is curious about and gets into *everything*.

Were you expecting your baby to fit right in with your own system of values and to confirm your sense of who *you* are? Problems can arise if you misinterpret the lack of fit as a rejection of your parenting, your values, yourself. A lack of fit is no reflection on your adequacy as a parent. If your baby's personality conflicts with your own so much that you feel basically at odds, this will place you under increased stress and require you to find additional ways of coping. This struggle to cope and to run counter to your own personality in order to be responsive to your baby can raise questions about your adequacy as a parent. If you could monitor your expectation that you would feel quite in harmony with your baby, you may be better able to reassure yourself when the self-doubts crop up again.

Another reason for your deciding to have a baby may have involved a wish to express or strengthen the commitment you and your partner feel toward each other. At least the five other new-parent couples touring with you all felt that their decision to have a baby depended to some extent on their experiencing a feeling of commitment to each other. Thus, Bob explained that in resolving his concerns about undertaking this additional financial responsibility, "I didn't have real serious hesitations; I wasn't worried about our relationship . . . I wasn't worried about *us*." And even when the decision to have the baby was made subsequent to conception, Ed reasoned, "We knew that we were ready together—I mean, we were committed to each other."

Again, these examples are not necessarily to be understood as exemplary, but they may help you to get more in touch with your own situation. Did you feel a similar sense of commitment between yourself and your partner that entered into your decision to have a baby? How solid a commitment do you feel you have to one another or want to have?

The divorce rate, which seems to be rising all around, is not exactly a state secret. It may well cause a person to wonder just how long his or her current relationship is destined to last. One could welcome the freedom and flexibility this allows, the knowledge that one isn't trapped and there certainly is a way out. Yet the impermanence could still be disconcerting and stimulate wishes for a greater sense of security. So some part of the couples' feeling of commitment described above—and maybe felt by you as well—may reflect the *wish* for permanency and security in relationships. And what could be more permanent than parenthood?

A rather extreme example is the anonymous couple who are having some serious difficulties in their relationship and seek to correct or camouflage their basic problems, that is, stabilize their partnership, by having a baby. Perhaps you've encountered such a couple, who one minute seem on the brink of splitting up and the next minute seem to shed their problems in a kind of honeymoon phase of expectancy, as they await their new little savior. But their baby turns out to be no miracle worker. In fact, the baby is beginning life with the serious handicap of being a basic disappointment in meeting the parents' specific expectation of healing their troubled relationship. How is the baby going to be able to feel pleasing, quite good-enough? And what can the

disappointed parents do for the baby and for themselves?
All is certainly not lost if the situation can be recognized for what it is. The parents need to be able to identify and give credit to their original wish—namely, a wish to stabilize their relationship by getting some basic problems fixed or at least put aside. It is neither appropriate nor possible to turn to a baby for the kind of help they need. They should, rather, seek out a wise man or woman, a professional offering frank sense, to help them sort out what is going on between them. (See the chapter "Who Cares About Parents, Anyway?")

Often secret expectations embedded in the reasons for deciding to have a baby are reflected in the name(s) chosen for the new family member. Your choice of name(s) for your baby probably was the result of a whole process you and your partner went through, since the two of you are unlikely to have reached immediate agreement on all of the following:

—a girl's first name,
—a boy's first name,
—a girl's middle name (or none),
—a boy's middle name (or none),
—what nickname would be used for a girl,
—what nickname would be used for a boy,
—what nickname would definitely *not* be used for a girl,
—what nickname would definitely *not* be used for a boy.
—a last name, in cases where the woman wants to keep
  her family name.

Perhaps you found yourself agreeing to discard names you liked in deference to your partner's tastes. Perhaps you exercised some veto power yourself at some names your partner suggested. Maybe you agreed that the mom-to-be would have more weight in deciding a girl's name and the dad-to-be would have the edge in selecting a boy's name, or vice versa.

What's in a name, anyway? Did you simply like the

sound of the name(s) you picked, free of any association? Or did you name your baby after someone:

—yourself,
—your partner,
—your grandfather,
—your partner's elderly rich aunt,
—an esteemed mentor,
—a childhood friend,
—a favorite storybook character,
—a current hero(ine) of yours,
—a cute little kid you once met?

The options are endless. The point is that the name(s) you chose for your baby may well carry with it (them) certain expectations you have for your baby:

—as a baby, child, or adult,
—as a future brilliant, creative, or otherwise wondrous person,
—as a friend or companion to you,
—to be a means of pleasing your parents or grandparents,
—to be a means of expressing gratitude toward a mentor or your partner,
—to be a memorial to someone dear to you, to some special relationship from your past, to some piece of you long ago,
—to be or do something "beyond" who you are, what you have done.

These expectations may relate to your reasons for deciding to have a baby in the first place.

How do you feel your baby is living up to these expectations you had? Think about whether your expectations are such that:

—your baby will be likely to meet them well enough just by being there, merely by existing,
—your baby must be a certain way to meet your expectations, so that you are likely to be conditionally pleased

with your baby,
—your baby, in reality, could not hope to live up to the
expectations you had in mind.

Now is a good time for you and your partner to think
through your expectations and discuss them with each
other. Clearly, they will affect your parenting and the
messages you give your baby. You want to do what you
can to avoid weighting your baby down with preformed
expectations that could stifle his or her innate potentials.
After all, isn't it true that what you *really* want your baby
to have is the freedom to develop his or her own potentials—regardless of your expectations?

So gaining perspective on this historical site of your
decision to have a baby is important work, as it's crucial
in safeguarding the unique potentials of your baby. The
next chapter focuses more on the history of your less-
immediate past. But before digging into this, you might
want to flip through some photographs from your childhood to set the mood.

Once Upon Your Moms and Dads

The last chapter concluded your tour of your immediate pre-parenthood past—labor and delivery, pregnancy, and your decision to have a baby. By now all this recent history of yours probably seems quite relevant to you in your current situation. This chapter invites you to continue your tour by looking even farther back, to your own childhood. The parenting you experienced back then has bearing on how your own parenthood is unfolding.

You may recall having vowed at least once as you were growing up, that if *you* ever got to be a parent you wouldn't do with any child of yours what your mom or dad was doing with you right then. So now maybe you are readying yourself to carry out those vows, to do things differently, to become a self-made parent.

That would certainly fit agreeably with the way you have proposed to run your own life. For example, before you even decided to have this baby you singled out (and were singled out by) your partner. Surely you intended this developing relationship to offer more than a mirror image of your parents' marriage. And before that, when you were a teenager, you probably set out to be different from either of your parents, an individual in your own right.

Nevertheless, your own family of origin was your starting point. And so, in deciding to have a baby and/or in anticipating this arrival, you may well have thought back on this start, the parenting you received. You may have tried to sort it out a bit. There are qualities, attitudes, and behaviors you attribute to one or the other of your parents that you feel were helpful to you in growing up. You perceive other attributes of theirs as having been unhelpful, perhaps even traumatizing.

As a new parent, you surely want to do things your own way, but not *merely* to be a self-made parent, different from your own mom and dad. What you would really like, after all, is to be a *better* parent, unlimited by what you feel were your parents' shortcomings. But to do this, surely you need not discard the good-enough aspects of your mom's and dad's parenting just to be different.

It makes sense, then, to try to think first about what your parents seemed to do right or well enough. These are attitudes and behaviors which you as a parent want to be able to repeat and expand upon.

In assessing what went "right" in the way your parents responded to you, consider whether you have an overall feeling that you are quite good-enough as a person—that you didn't turn out so badly, after all. If so, some rather crucial basic parenting must have gone "right" early in your life, even if you can't identify the specifics. They may include such strengths as:

—your mother's or father's concern for you,
—your parents' concern for each other,
—your mother's or father's openness and honesty about feelings,
—your mother's or father's affection toward you,
—the affection your parents expressed toward each other,
—your mother's or father's calm,
—your mother's or father's reasonableness, fairness,
—your mother's or father's disciplinary ideas and actions,
—your mother's or father's respect for you as an individual,
—your parents' respect for each other as individuals.

Besides assessing what your parents did "right" with you, you need to be able to reject and move on from whatever you've experienced as your parents' "mistakes":

—too little of any of the strengths listed above,

—too much concern (to the point of raising unnecessary worries about one's very safety),

—too much expressed affection (to the point of being sexually over-stimulating),

—too much calm or reasonableness (to the point of withholding emotional responses),

—too much discipline (to the point of denying deserved praise or discouraging creativity),

—a striking inconsistency and unpredictability in the degree to which any of the above qualities were put into practice.

Taking stock this way is not for the purpose of finding fault with or blaming your parents. That would not be helpful. What's more, your parents did the best job they were able to do. After all, they had parents, too. And their parents could only have done their best, having been imperfectly parented themselves . . . and so on. So the aim of assessing the parenting you received is not to assign blame but to exercise the old All-American Freedom of Choice in regard to what you repeat and what you reject. Indeed, you intend to express your individuality through your own blend of parenting. This includes making your *own* mistakes, if you must make mistakes at all.

Unfortunately, though, it's not that easy to make your own free choices and put them into action. Your past exerts a particularly strong opposing pull. Certain patterns have been set up, beginning early in your family of origin. This past may seem quite distant to you now. The tour of your more recent pre-parenthood past may appear more relevant to you.

But even your long, long ago is on the continuum of your life and so has supplied some constants that live on as parts of who you are today. Like it or not, everyone has a tendency to repeat early experiences. And new parents are no exceptions. As you have been noting, your own perceptions and behaviors as new parents tend to follow earlier patterns. Moreover, parents commonly (and most often unintentionally) recreate for their children some form of their own growing-up experiences. This recreating tends to be an automatic and rather indiscriminate repetition of both positively- and negatively-experienced childhood events and family interactions.

No malice is intended, you understand, when you repeat a pattern that you have perceived as negative. Rather, it is a quite unconscious means of seizing another opportunity for dealing with and (at last!) mastering something that resulted in emotional distress long ago. The unconscious wish is that *this* time around, you will cope more effectively and therefore with less trauma than was possible when in a similar situation as a child.

But, of course, you would like to break out of the "mistake" cycles, which tend to be handed down from generation to generation. To interrupt this cycle you must be able to recognize times when you are falling into the automatic position and repeating some "mistake" pattern. You can't expect this recognition to come quickly or easily. But you will be more likely to recognize your own automatically repeating "mistake" cycles if you are convinced of and challenged by the thoughts that:

—repetitions echo down from past to present and future generations;

—the process of repetition is oh-so tenacious;

—most likely the repeating patterns will tend to recur with you;

—in essence, you would be defying your own unconscious by recognizing the patterns on a conscious level;

—you are not in the most objective position for observing your own patterns, so they probably won't be

readily apparent to you;
—you will need to be a detective, alert and active in un-
covering clues if you hope to become aware of your
own patterns;
—this endeavor could prove very worthwhile: interesting and revealing to you, beneficial to your baby, and
enhancing to healthy development of relationships in
your new family.

All this pattern-finding is surely easier to accomplish
in theory than in reality. It's true that the experiences of
your early years get stirred up, reactivated at some level,
just by having a child of your own who is now embark-
ing on those same early years. But your memory of your
own childhood may be anywhere from altogether vague
to unusually clear. You may have only the fuzziest
impressions about such details as your parents' various
attitudes and behaviors back then. Or you may have a
distinct picture of your early experiences. Whether you
feel somewhat vague about such impressions or awash
in a sea of details, you may be better able to make sense
of your childhood experiences by focusing on specific
questions, such as:

—How was affection expressed in your family?
—How was anger handled?
—Who disciplined you, and in what ways?

The point is to stimulate your memories and order your
thoughts in your search for past patterns that you may
be likely to repeat.

More specifically still, as you grew up, you intimately
experienced and learned one primary example of what a
biological father or mother feels, believes, and does. Now
that you are a father or mother yourself, it would be
most relevant to your own development as a parent to
reflect upon your sense of that parent who is the same
sex you are. (Your sense of your other parent is also relevant, but perhaps more so in terms of the expectations

you may have of your partner as a parent to your child than in terms of the first-hand relationship you are developing with your new family member.)

Now, as your tourmates bid you farewell, they leave you one final set of examples from their personal experiences to help guide this last portion of your tour, to give you practice in a more objective position than you could have in looking only at your own experiences. Each of the following examples has been extracted from a whole labyrinth of personal reflections. Each is presented to you as a distilled version of the impressions your tourmates individually shared about that parent of his or hers who (being of the same sex) has served most directly as a role model for that person.

There is a recurrent theme among the experiences reported by the other fathers who are on this tour with you and your partner. Each one felt that his own father was more distant with him than he hopes to be with his own child. Bob's story seems typical in this way:

> My father didn't have a lot of input. . . . He wasn't around a tremendous amount when we were real young, and I don't think he really knows how to deal with children. . . . He had a hard time showing affection.

Frank elaborated further:

> My father worked hard during life and he didn't have much time for us as children. You know, when he came home, he regarded home more as a refuge, and children didn't enter into, like having time and, you know, playing with us and so forth. . . . So he was very much to me like a distant kind of person who was there to come down on you if you did wrong, but really you didn't have much interaction with him on other levels. . . . I remember my own childhood: I always wished that I could get more

attention from my father. . . . I would like to spend a lot of time, to the extent possible, with my child . . . so he gets to know me as a person, and to be supportive and not critical—not regard him as a threat to my inner peace here, but as a human being who is growing regardless, just 'cause he's there, just 'cause I wanted him in the world.

The wish Frank expressed—that his child get to know him as a person—is highlighted by the reports of the three other fathers on your tour. Dan, Ed, and Curt all saw their fathers as tending to "go along with" their mothers in family matters. They seemed to feel that the lack of direct input from their fathers gave their mothers license to be intrusive and controlling over them to the point where their own sense of privacy—and even identity—was at risk.

Ed's efforts to stake out his own identity, quite separate from that of his parents, have contributed to his choosing both a partner and a lifestyle that differ from any his parents would find acceptable. In making these choices, he seems to be courting his parents' rejection. In this way he is managing to perpetuate a pattern of his father's:

Now, my father was rejected by his family, or rejected them. I mean, he just hasn't spoken to them in years. . . . He's rejecting now. I mean, he wrote me a letter that said, "Goodbye, Ed."

Curt has attempted to counteract the model of his "overly distant" father by selecting another model. He feels he was partly attracted to Cathy in high school because "she had a very neat family. I really enjoyed her family." Since his teenage years Curt has had a relationship with Cathy's father, a man who, Curt feels, enjoys a wonderfully close father-daughter relationship. Thus, Cathy's father offers Curt something of an alternative to his own father as a role model.

Curt is unusually lucky to have found a role model in a father-in-law who, way back when he was a young dad, was able to go counter to traditional role expectations and form a close, firsthand relationship with his baby. But clearly there are other new fathers nowadays who want to shift toward such a relationship with their babies. Your local chapter of the Parental Community might be a likely forum for exploring this new direction with others. Sharing ideas about a broader range of possible parent-child relationship patterns could lead to your developing alternatives to the one pattern you experienced yourself as a child.

The five mothers who are accompanying you and your partner on this tour are also having difficulties accepting their own mothers as models for them in their new role. Cathy thinks of her mother as not very affectionate, and she believes her mother must have been unhappy and uncomfortable nurturing babies—quite contrary to how Cathy feels she is herself. She explained:

> We have a rather conflicting relationship. She doesn't feel as good, I think, about her parenting. The parenting she received was terrible and the parenting she gave wasn't the greatest, either. . . . I think she wrote me a letter saying something like she thought that I would do better than she did, or something.

Barb's perception is that her mother has "a tendency to get a little hysterical." In general, she feels her mother offers few useful guidelines because "typically my mother would say, 'Do whatever you want.'"

Both Barb and Cathy feel their mothers-in-law present themselves as having been all-time perfect mothers. Rather than considering them as alternative role models, both Barb and Cathy see these other mother figures as critical of them, discouraging and frustrating their efforts to cope with the new demands of parenthood. Barb mimicked her mother-in-law:

> "Oh, my kid never spit up. My kids never did it.
> They were perfect. They never got sick."

And Cathy quoted her mother-in-law:

> "Curt never cried during his whole infancy—no,
> once, I think. . . . And he slept through the night
> at age one week. . . . And he was toilet trained at
> six months. . . ." So when they were here and Cindy
> cried, they would immediately think it was some-
> thing we did wrong.

Fern, Erin, and Deirdre all have been acutely aware
for quite some time that they wanted to avoid repeating
their mothers' patterns. Each of them happens to have
experienced an extreme set of circumstances while
growing up. Fern reported feeling that, all along, friction
between her parents had "colored everything else." In
recent years their conflict ended in her father's killing her
mother and himself. Fern said that one of her reactions
to this event was such a strong wish to arrange her own
life differently that she then decided to divorce her first
husband and not be married. She recognizes that she
still gets frightened by her own angry feelings and needs
to remind herself that verbal outlets can be safe, that
fights surely can occur without ever becoming physical
battles.

Erin described her own mother as having been "a sad,
kind of insecure person," who left Erin with her grandmother right after she was born. Eleven years later Erin's
brother was born, and he, too, was left with the grandmother. But when Erin was in high school her grandmother became ill, and her mother

> . . . dumped him on *me*. . . . That was terrible. I
> hated him a lot. . . . I used to feel really guilty about,
> about not wanting to be his mother, you know,

(laugh), until I realized that I didn't have to *be* his mother; he wasn't my kid. . . . I'm sure it has a lot to do with why I postponed being a mother for so long, 'cause I was a mother for years, and I didn't even know it, you know, didn't even want it.

Because of her perceptions about her mother's lack of caretaking, and because of her own feelings about her brother, Erin, in the normal course of her own mothering, may come to feel "put upon" at times. She may then experience an exaggerated response of guilt all over again. If she can see how her current situation might be stirring up old feelings about having had to care for her brother, she will be more likely to view her present as different from her past circumstances. She might then be better able to accept whatever is happening in the present for what it is—simply an undesirable by-product of the role which in general she desires and which, *this time*, she chose to take on.

Deirdre's mother had always told her how she hated everything about being a mother and how all four of her children were "accidents." Deirdre grew up feeling that for her to have children would mean, paradoxically, that she was being disloyal to her own mother. This conflict had prompted her to seek professional help. She is convinced that psychotherapy has allowed her to have a different experience as a mother, neither repeating her own mother's pattern nor avoiding motherhood altogether.

If you can be aware of how things were for you as a child in your original family, you are in a better position to monitor how things develop in your new family. You wouldn't want to become overly self-conscious, however, so concerned about what patterns you may be repeating that you inhibit your own responses to your new family member. It is important for you to react to your baby spontaneously, with feeling—not only with thinking, which requires at least some preliminary pause.

But some parental feeling responses may be counter-productive, not what you want. And some may feel all too familiar, sending signals echoing through time that herein lies a pattern. You then may want to think about why these feeling responses might be rather stubborn. If you can figure out what purpose(s) they serve, you will be freer to consider other possible responses, and perhaps react differently in the future.

For example, you may notice that you feel upset whenever your partner spends what seems like a long time alone with your baby. You may even recognize that you feel jealous. You try to remember when you felt like that before, say when you were a child. Maybe you can recall your mom and dad going off somewhere alone together—without you. Or perhaps you remember how it felt being put to bed, knowing that your parents would still be keeping each other company. Or your perception may be that one of your parents (possibly the one who happens to be the same sex you are) seemed to feel left out and get upset at times when you and your other parent were alone with each other. Once you under-stand what pattern is being repeated, you can consider ways to keep from feeling excluded in your current sit-uation by:

—participating more with your baby yourself, and by appreciating how special your own brand of relating is;
—being present more often when your partner needs to spend time with your baby, learning how different your partner's style is from your own and how important each of you is to your baby;
—saving time to continue to be alone with your partner, preserving the specialness of your adult relationship;
—talking with your partner about your feelings so as to get some help with monitoring them and eventually interrupting the pattern.

Another example: You find yourself feeling increasingly impatient with your baby's helplessness. You may think back on how much your own parents seemed to value your growing independence, your achieving things *on your own*. You may even wonder if there ever was a time when they were comfortable allowing you to be dependent on them, helpless to do anything for yourself, by yourself. . . . Maybe when you were physically ill . . . Yet surely there were other times when it would have felt good to have had their active support and help, to have believed it was okay with them for you to use them to feel less all alone. If, on the contrary, you sensed that your parents were likely to look with disfavor upon any such dependence on your part, you can understand that you may have mixed feelings about your baby's dependence on you: Rationally, you might want to foster this dependency, while at the same time you might feel put off by your baby's helplessness and unintentionally react with impatience. It is extremely difficult to give anyone, even your own baby, the emotional support that you feel was withheld from you early in life. Although you cannot go back and truly make up for an early emotional deficit, you can hope to work out a relationship with your partner that meets some of your current emotional needs. If your own needs are being met, you are far more likely to be able to meet your baby's needs. So perhaps you can allow your partner to contribute to your parenting capacities by:

—doing certain tasks for you,
—sharing problems and the responsibility for working out solutions together,
—listening to you,
—understanding you,
—reassuring you that you are cared about,
—just plain holding you.

From time to time you may want to make sure that the

dependence such interactions imply really is okay with your partner. You may need to remind yourself that it is appropriate for your relationship to be mutual and for your partner to be similarly dependent on you at times. Together, then, you could discuss and monitor any growing impatience either of you may have in response to your baby's dependency. And you might just begin to feel better cared for yourself and, in turn, more able to care for your baby.

And a final example: You find yourself feeling acutely worried about your baby's safety. You fear that something awful is going to befall your baby. Perhaps feelings connected with some important earlier loss—say the death or extended hospitalization of your own father or mother—are getting stirred up anew. In this case you need to reassure yourself somehow that the loss is not going to be repeated, that the present situation is in fact separate and different from the earlier one. And/or it may be that the anxiety you feel stems from your anger at your baby—the extent and constancy of the demands— and your wish that something would happen to get you out of this situation. Here, too, you had better reassure yourself that wishes are quite different from actions and that these are wishes you are not about to act out.

But, more than that, you need to make sure you are getting enough relief from all the baby demands. This may mean developing some creative plan like taking care of someone else's child at times so that the other parent will be available to step in for you when you need a break. Again, perhaps your partner can help you monitor your own reactions.

Perhaps, as you think about how things were for you growing up in your family, you become aware of other patterns you intend to alter in your new three-person family. Maybe you plan to:

—express affection or anger more comfortably than you

felt your parents were able to do,
—discipline your child more rationally than you felt your
mother or father disciplined you,
—place more realistic or more constructive (or at least
different) expectations on your child than you sense
your parents placed on you,
—enlist your partner's assistance
   —in observing your ongoing interactions with your
   baby,
   —in thinking about and discussing the meanings and
   repercussions of your interactions,
   —in formulating and experimenting with alternative
   responses to your baby.

Enlisting your partner's assistance with such monitoring requires a relationship built rather solidly on a basis of trust. Since the pattern being monitored is one which you have agreed would be better left behind, you could feel uncomfortable, defensive, or even "accused" by your partner when attention is called to the pattern's being repeated. It takes trust to feel sure that your partner will try to be helpful and will keep these discussions as confidential as you wish them to be. It takes trust to know that at no time (not immediately and not in the future) will your partner use observations and understandings of your patterns for unconstructive ends (for example, to criticize or angrily humiliate you).

Mutual trust is necessary, but it's not sufficient by itself. To prepare for such monitoring you and your partner might also anticipate just how and when you could most constructively call the other's attention to those potentially sensitive behaviors and attitudes which you had agreed might be worth flagging for one another.

Knowing your partner and your particular relationship, you may want to discuss your observations the moment you make them, regardless of where you happen to be or what else is occurring at the time. Or it might be easier to gain a constructive perspective

—later, in the hope of altering reactions in similar future situations, rather than attempting to halt a reaction, mid-stream;
—when you and your partner are alone and relatively free of distractions;
—if you first check on whether you both feel up to a possibly "heavy" discussion right then, or whether you are likely to have a better opportunity very soon (make a date!).

In other words, even if you have made such a monitoring arrangement, you'll want to be sensitive to how receptive you and your partner may be to follow-up discussions at any given time.

To illustrate how such monitoring might be sensitively handled, consider the following imaginary scenario:

She and He had previously talked about the tendency of his family *never* to say anything negative about any family member. They both had agreed that they would not want to perpetuate this repressive tradition with their children. But this evening at dinner with his parents, She was sure that He cringed uncomfortably and frowned at her warningly when She mentioned that his brother's kid had frightened their baby by playing too roughly yesterday. She waited until his parents were gone, the baby was asleep for the night, and She and He were alone.

She: Can we talk for a few minutes before we turn in?

He: Gee, I'm pretty tired. . . .

She: I know you've had a long day, Hon, but I felt real upset for awhile at dinner tonight and I think I'd feel a lot better if we could discuss it just a bit. . . .

He: Sure, I wasn't aware that you were upset. What about?

She: Well, when I started to talk about your nephew, you seemed annoyed, angry, like you wanted me to shut up.

He: Well, I guess I thought you were upsetting Mom and Dad unnecessarily. But it wasn't that big a deal. I mean, I didn't intend to upset you.

She: I know. And it's not that you have to like or agree with everything I say . . . it's just that I felt like you were automatically wanting to cover up family imperfections like your parents do, and I was real uneasy about your doing that.

He: (Pause.) I guess a kind of don't-make-waves reflex did kick into action.

She: You're right that it wasn't so big a deal in itself. . . . I think I just got worried that you might keep up your parents' pattern of glossing over family unpleasantness, and it feels almost dishonest.

He: I s'pose I've gotten used to not saying certain things around my folks. But I certainly don't want to do that with you or with Pumpkin. So if you feel it carries over to us, I really do want you to let me know right away.

She: Okay. Thanks. . . . I do feel better.

If you cannot imagine having a similar kind of conversation with your partner, keep in mind that communication is partly a matter of practice, combined with a mutual willingness to make the effort. But should you feel that too much would be risked by communicating so openly, then you might wonder how much you and your partner actually trust each other—and how much trust you would like to have in your relationship.

You might also take time to wonder whether some pattern of closed lines of communication is being repeated from your childhood family. The next chapter contains guidelines on more open communication.

Who Cares About Parents, Anyway?

People laugh at W. C. Fields' claim that anyone who hates dogs and small children can't be all bad. But even W. C. Fields did not go so far as to knock babies. That wouldn't be funny; it would be blasphemous. After all, babies are never a nuisance, are they? No, babies are just cute and cuddly; they are fun and gratifying to care for and about. Everyone cares about babies. At least, everyone you care about now cares about your baby.

Your pediatrician, your neighbors, your friends, your relatives. They see you or talk on the phone with you and they ask about your baby. Not long ago your mother or your mother-in-law, or both, regularly used to check in to see how you were, what was new with you, what you and your partner had been doing or were planning to do. Now the callers by-pass how *you* are, what *you* are doing. Instead they ask about your baby, what developmental wonders—or worries—are the news of the hour. Even your grandmother or your favorite aunt or uncle—who always has made you feel so very special—now wants to know first about your baby. Congratulatory gifts arrive at your door for the baby. It is a rare friend or colleague—and usually a non-parent at that—who sees fit to acknowledge your baby's birth with a gift for *you* as a person rather than strictly for you as a parent. At least, chances are that you have not received, say, a comfortable pair of slippers, or a novel you might read for fun, or (perish the thought!) a sexy cologne or aftershave, in honor of the momentous occasion of becoming a parent.

All of which is quite fine with you, really. You aren't exactly feeling by-passed since it's your baby who's being acknowledged. And your baby at this stage feels like part of you, a deeply meaningful part.

But still only part. You are more than a parent, just as you are more than a spouse; more than a person who works at a particular job; more than a jogger or a puzzle-worker or a music lover or a sports enthusiast or a barb-quer or a bird-watcher; more than a consumer or neighbor or friend or relative. The complex combination of specifics that identifies you cannot be distilled down to one or even a few characteristics of role, culture, personality, socioeconomic status, age, and gender. "Parent," then, is an incomplete title. You are more than your relationship to your baby.

Amid all the delight and concern and discussions and oohing and ahing over your new family member, it is important to keep yourself—your whole self—in perspective. It would be all too easy to get completely caught up in caring for your baby and for yourself only insofar as you are your baby's caretaker.

Who cares about the new parent as a person? Well, the first answer is the new parent himself or herself. You, as a new parent, need to care about yourself as a person. All your roles and activities and relationships require your energy and care. Only if you are cared about and for, only if your needs are met in basic ways, can you hope to meet the needs of your baby, let alone to go on filling other non-parent roles that still are meaningful to you—as spouse, neighbor, friend, child, grandchild. And you're the one in the best position to be aware of what you need and to make sure your needs are met. Only you can really be consistently in touch with your own needs.

In the abstract, it is easy to understand and appreciate that everyone, even parents, have needs—yourself included. But since you have become a parent, your adult status seems to be in stark contrast to your infant's state of being entitled to have every need met. So you must remind yourself in your busyness of caring for your new baby that you are entitled to recognize and acknowledge your own needs as well. You, too, need to feel support from others, to be cared about and even cared for. Moreover, you are entitled to communicate these needs to others, not to wail out demands or thrash about until pacified regardless of what you want, but to negotiate on your own behalf in an adult and straightforward manner.

This negotiating occurs within a relationship—with your partner, for example. Principles of negotiation also can be applied in relationships with other relatives, friends, neighbors, co-workers, employers, employees. The following ten steps are essentially the same whenever you as an adult ask something from another person:

—First, you recognize how you feel.

—Second, you become clear about what you want or need, what you think would help you feel better.

—Third, you share *in words* how you feel, taking particular care to avoid placing blame on or sounding accusing toward your partner (since accusations only stimulate return accusations).

—Fourth, you make or be prepared to make a specific request.

—Fifth, you remain open to discussion, to alternate solutions.

—Sixth, you acknowledge your partner's position and needs (which at times conflict with your own).

—Seventh, you ask or suggest how you might be helpful in return.

—Eighth, you realize that compromises might be necessary, possible, and good enough.

—Ninth, you give due credit for whatever help, efforts, or understanding your partner offers you in response.

—Finally, you keep in mind that:
  —negotiating takes practice;
  —every negotiation does not necessarily end with a
    bargain, agreement, or even an "okay" deal;
  —the communication itself can be important for your
    relationship, whatever the particular result;
  —there will be plenty of other opportunities for initi-
    ating and responding to negotiations with your
    partner.

To demonstrate how you can use these steps, imagine this hypothetical situation: You have just put in a hectic, frustrating day; you have dealt with one unexpected crisis after another, and now your baby is crying. According to the understood or explicit arrangement you have with your partner, you're the one who is supposed to be on call.

First, silently, you recognize how you feel: exhausted, put-upon, unhelped, maybe even resentful and angry.

Second, still silently, you try to sort out what you want, what might help you feel better: if your baby would drop off to sleep right away (which doesn't sound likely!); if your partner would bring the baby to you or, better yet, take care of the baby for you this time; if your partner would take care of you a bit while you tend the baby, by getting you a snack or something to drink, by sitting and talking with you while you do the changing and feeding; or simply by acknowledging how much you've had to deal with all day.

Third, you open the conversation, telling your partner, "Oh, I feel like I haven't much energy left for the baby today. It feels like all day one thing after another's gone wrong."

Fourth, you request, "I know I'm supposed to take care of this screaming, but would you take over this time, dear?

Fifth, you listen and consider alternatives as your partner responds, "Aw, come on. I've had a hard day, too, you know. I was just hoping to relax, unwind a bit, read the paper."

Sixth, you acknowledge what you've heard, saying, "I know. I'm sure your day was no picnic. I guess I just don't want to feel like I'm continuing to carry the ball all alone now. Would you be willing to keep me company, while I get our favorite screamer settled down?"

Seventh, you point out some pay-off for your partner, offering, "Then I'd be able to listen to what you were trying to tell me earlier about the carpenter's estimate."

Eighth, if you and your partner reach an agreement, you feel the compromise will be good enough; and

Ninth, you express appreciation, "Thanks for understanding; it helps that you're here."

Finally, if your partner turns down your request, you exercise whatever self-discipline is required to avoid placing blame (or calling names). You still say how you feel, "I'm disappointed. But I'm still glad you listened. I don't know why, but it's important to me that you know how rough a day I had. And maybe next time we'll figure out a way for *both* of us to get more or less what we feel we need."

Negotiating does take practice. So perhaps one further example would help you feel more familiar with the suggested steps in this process. Consider the following scenario: Your baby is being fed exclusively by his or her mother; you have suddenly realized that it feels very important to you that your baby begin to have close connections with his or her father as well as with mother.

As Father

First, silently, you recognize how you feel:
left out of your baby's involvement with your partner. You wish things were more even and that your baby were involved with you, too.

Second, still silently, you try to sort out what might help you feel better.
You realize that:
—you had agreed that your partner would be the main caretaker for your baby;
—you have limited amounts of time and energy, given all your other responsibilities;
—giving your baby a bottle, say, two or three times a week, would encourage you and your baby to be more involved with each other, without either taking up too much time or inter-rupting your plan that your partner be the main caretaker.

Third, you open the conversa-tion, telling your partner, "I've been having some feelings about our plan for the baby's care that I hadn't

As Mother

First, silently, you recognize how you feel:
sad that your baby and your partner are not getting the chance to share feeding times. You're sure they'd both enjoy this closeness.

Second, still silently, you try to sort out what might help you feel better.
You realize that:
—you had agreed to be the main caretaker for your baby;
—your partner has limited amounts of time and energy, given all his other responsibilities;
—giving your baby a bottle, say, two or three times a week would encourage your partner and your baby to be more involved with each other, without either taking up much time or interrupting the plan that you be the main caretaker.

Third, you open the conversa-tion, telling your partner, "I've been having some feelings about our plan for the baby's care that I hadn't counted on."

Fourth, you make a specific

counted on."

Fourth, you make a specific request: "I think I'd like to share some of the feedings with you; that would get the baby-and-daddy connection off to an even more special, early start."

Fifth, you listen and consider alternatives as your partner replies, "But what will that do to the nursing? People say to be sure to keep stimulating the breast milk supply with regular feedings. Besides, there's always the possibility of giving bottles of water between feedings."

Sixth, you acknowledge what you've heard, responding, "I know, I know. But the water doesn't seem to be very interesting or satisfying—How do babies learn so fast that there is something better, anyway?—Well, I wouldn't want to do anything that might interrupt the milk supply. But perhaps some breast milk could be put into a bottle. That would keep the supply up and it'd even taste the same to the baby. Of course, we'd better plan for Mom to stick around for the first time,

request: "I think I'd like to share some of the feedings with you; that would get the baby-and-daddy connection off to an even more special, early start."

Fifth, you listen and consider alternatives as your partner replies, "But what will that do to the nursing? People say to be sure to keep stimulating the breast milk supply with regular feedings. Besides, there's always the possibility of giving bottles of water between feedings."

Sixth, you acknowledge what you've heard, responding, "I know, I know. But the water doesn't seem to be very interesting or satisfying—How do babies learn so fast that there is something better, anyway?—Well, I wouldn't want to do anything that might interrupt the milk supply. But perhaps some breast milk could be put into a bottle. That would keep the supply up and it'd even taste the same to the baby. Of course, we'd better plan for Mom to stick around for the first time, just in case some coaching might be wanted."

just in case some coaching might be wanted."

Seventh, you add some incentive, pointing out, "If this goes well, you can have longer stretches for breaks, go out on your own, through a feeding."

Eighth, if you get the message that compromise is needed, you offer, "I'd be glad to try to get you one of those new negative-suction breast pumps the nurse at the hospital was saying are so easy and comfortable to use."

Ninth, you express your appreciation, "Thanks for understanding my change of heart about wanting to share some feedings with you."

Tenth, if your partner remains unwilling or unable to compromise, you try to leave the door open to future negotiation, suggesting
—"You can take your time and think about it further."
—"I'd be interested in hearing more about your hesitations."
—"Maybe we could talk this over with some other couples who use supplementary bottles."

Seventh, you add some incentive, pointing out, "If this goes well, you can have longer stretches for you and baby to be alone together, get to know each other better."

Eighth, if you get the message that compromise is needed, you offer, "I'd stay around as long as you'd want me to, but I was thinking that I could run one or two of your errands for you if I'd have enough time to go downtown."

Ninth, you express your appreciation, "Thanks for understanding my change of heart about wanting to share some feedings with you."
Tenth, if your partner remains unwilling or unable to compromise, you try to leave the door open to future negotiation, suggesting
—"You can take your time and think about it further."
—"I'd be interested in hearing more about your hesitations."
—"Maybe we could talk this over with some other couples who use supplementary bottles."
—"Let's see how things go

—"Let's see how things go and plan to discuss it later; who knows, maybe some happy medium will occur to us by then."

So, to return to the question at hand—Who cares about you as a parent-person? First, you do. And second, hopefully, your partner does. You and your partner have ways of expressing your caring to each other, verbally and nonverbally. To a greater or lesser degree you trust your partner to care. The more you can trust that you and your partner are likely to respond to each other with mutual caring, the more open and honest your communication can be.

Again, you are not in search of a perfect relationship but one that is really good enough to allow you to be mutually supportive while you both grow separately and together. And sometimes establishing a truly vital relationship requires professional assistance. A baby can give a couple something to talk about but is helpless in fixing faulty communication or increasing the basis of trust between the parents. Professional assistance is necessary not only for the couple, but also for the baby's sake whenever the decision to have a child has been seen as the way to save or fix a floundering marriage.

Professional help is *essential*, too, if you ever become truly worried about being able to protect your baby from acts of anger or frustration (true abuse or neglect). Then it is imperative that you get some help *for yourself*. You are depleted. You need input. You are entitled to have someone care about *you*. Only then can you expect to have supplies, inner resources to call upon for parenting your baby.

The national organization called "Parents Anonymous" maintains groups of trained volunteers in local chapters throughout the country. These people are available to talk with you. Use them. Call and ask if they have a "Stress Hotline" for parents. Usually such a service is arranged so that you could maintain contact with one particular volunteer. You do not even have to give your name unless you want to do so. It is usually hardest to make the initial call, but once you manage to pick up the phone and make that first contact, you should experience some immediate relief in being able to do even that much for yourself and in simply being responded to by a caring adult. After that, it should seem easier to use this contact either in a continuing way, or as you feel it would be helpful to you.

Professional help can be extremely useful for other purposes, too:

—in opening up communication between partners, without either person placing blame on the other or feeling too vulnerable with the other;
—in pointing out reasons why counterproductive patterns of perceiving or relating to your partner or your baby developed and why they may have been so hard for you to change by yourself;
—in developing alternative ways of perceiving or relating to your partner or your baby;
—in adding perspective when you and your partner differ radically about your baby or your parenting roles;
—in coping with special situations: a premature birth, multiple births, a baby with birth defects or chronic illness, unresolved feelings about an earlier loss of some family member.

You probably put some stock in the tradition that praises independence, prizes "making it" on your own—the tradition of Daniel Boone's hacking his way through the wilderness by himself, of George Washington Carver's pulling himself up by his own bootstraps, of Emily Dickinson's creative solitude. Typical American attitudes attest to a reverence for those who are "self-made," an appreciation for today's do-it-yourself enthusiasts. But ask yourself seriously what real advantage(s) you get from always sorting out everything on your own. Explorers, scientists, writers, all surely take advantage of whatever tools and methods are available and useful to them. So if at times a professional's input would be useful to you (personally or in your relationship with your partner or your baby), why not take advantage of the availability of that tool?

Professionals who consult with couples are tools available for you to use if and when you could do with a bit of help in sorting out your relationship. They won't make decisions for you. Rather, they'll offer new ways for you to look at what's going on, allowing you to find (and choose, or not choose) alternative ways of handling things.

But *who* might be useful to you and *how* might you find competent and appropriate professionals? Titles alone are unreliable, since there are competent (and incompetent) people who call themselves marriage counselors, family therapists, sex therapists, psychotherapists—titles which can belong to people in any of a number of recognized professions, or in no organized profession at all. Even licensed professionals—social workers, psychologists, medical doctors, psychiatrists—have varying degrees of competence in dealing with those particular issues which might be of concern to you. And, as you know, there is no one sure-fire way to get a good referral.

Probably the most common referral sources are:

—friends who have been helped by a particular professional. (If the source is a close friend, getting a referral from the professional may be more appropriate than seeking help directly from this same person. Surely competent professionals should know and refer to others who are also competent.)
—the out-patient psychiatric unit of a respected general

hospital in your area. (Perhaps help is available there, in which case find out right away how long a wait you would face there. Alternatively, the intake worker might recommend two or three persons elsewhere who would be appropriate for the particular concerns you have.)

—your internist, obstetrician or pediatrician. (If the medical doctor you consult seems to downplay your concerns as "normal," "temporary," or "unfounded," you can remind yourself that new parenthood is indeed an unusually anxious stage. Nonetheless, your concerns are worthy of attention and if they remain after being pronounced "normal," you might approach your doctor again with a very clear and direct request: For example, "Doctor, I'd like your help. I know you think I'm over-reacting about _____, but I still feel really upset about it and would like to talk with someone just to evaluate what's going on. I would feel better consulting someone you suggest to someone others might recommend. So I would very much appreciate it if you would give me a name or two I could call."

—the listing of practitioners published by the American Psychiatric Association, the American Psychological Association, the National Association of Social Workers, or—more immediately accessible—the yellow pages of the telephone book. (Those who let their fingers do the walking should use their heads while doing the talking.)

Actually, whatever your referral source, you will need to do your own evaluating, once you meet a professional you might use as a consultant. You can ask initial questions directly in your first contact with the consultant:

—Does the professional work with people who have concerns about _____?

—How much does the professional charge? (If relevant,

does your insurance policy cover this person's services—that is, what title, licensure does the professional have?)
—What is this professional's way of working with people having such concerns? Could you expect suggestions, discussion, listening? Might other members of your family be seen either separately or together with you?

You are after basic information. More than that, the responses you get will create an impression: Is this someone you feel you might be able to talk to? There probably is such a thing as a "fit," a match between patient and therapist, between parent and consultant. You could, of course, have such a match with many different professionals; there is not just one and only one "right" person for you. But there may be a number of competent consultants with whom you feel no "fit" would be possible for you. So you pay some attention to your own sense of how you and a potential consultant seem to respond to each other. You ask yourself whether:

—you might not feel hesitant no matter who your consultant,
—you might strongly prefer to talk to
  —a man or a woman,
  —someone younger or older,
  —someone of the same or a different race or religion,
—you might really care that the professional is or is not a parent also.

If none of these factors is an issue for you, fine. But if you are aware that it would be particularly uncomfortable—perhaps to the point of being nonproductive—to see a particular type of professional, you might try to avoid adding such an obstacle to those that you undoubtedly will encounter anyway.

The main point is that once you can recognize and acknowledge that you care about yourself, you may be able to approach others—your partner, your friends, your relatives, your doctors, your consultants—in ways that appropriately encourage their support and care for and about you. You are entitled.

You are entitled because you have become a parent, which is an important role indeed. But you are also entitled because you are still, first and foremost, a person.

Baby's Needs

Baby Talk

You are a verbal person. Years of mandatory education (and maybe more years after that) have impressed you with the importance and power of words. You have been instructed and graded in reading, writing, speaking, and figuring (which uses the symbolic language of mathematics). You may have taken "time out" from these primary subjects for art and music, but dance, theater, and concerted attention to sports probably were relegated to after school hours. The essential curriculum clearly aimed at developing your verbal skills.

And here you are, facing the peculiar, critical challenge of communicating nonverbally with your baby, learning to read the messages of a person who is without words, cannot yet even conceptualize in words, let alone talk to you and make specific requests. Might you by any chance feel a bit unprepared?

Part of the beauty of words is that they can be (or seem to be) so precise. True, they are open to interpretation and misinterpretation. By comparison, though, nonverbal communication seems inexact, impressionistic. You are called on to use all your senses to take in your baby's messages and to begin to sort out what they might mean.

You listen and hear all sorts of noises, from cries and coos to slight sleep-stirrings. You watch your baby's facial expression, body movements, skin color. You feel for temperature, heart rate (goodness but it's fast!), muscle tone—and if you're brave, for humidity. You sniff for odors—dirty diapers, burped milk, and underneath it all, the soft fresh scent of Newborn, the smell of your particular baby.

And you try to make sense out of all the information, the impressions your senses make available. How loud *is* that cry? (Of course, you must make allowances for the fact that the cry tends to seem louder, longer, more distressed and disruptive to that baby's parents—namely, to you—than to any others who may chance to be within earshot. Moreover, the cry may seem to you to signal more distress if there *are* others within range of hearing, others who you feel may judge your baby and/or you as a parent.) Just how much discomfort do you read in that particular intensity of cry? Where would it fall on the whimper-to-breathholding-scream scale?

WHIMPER	SQUIRM	FUSS	CRY	SCREAM:	RED	BLUE

1 2 3 4 5 6 7 8 9 10 11 12 13 14 15 16 17 18 19 20 21 22 23 24 25

Which is greater, your baby's discomfort or your own for not being sure what to do next?

Your mind ticks through the list of baby discomforts, checking off each possibility in turn:

Hungry?

—It's been only 43 minutes since the last feeding. Maybe last night's shorter feeding is now being felt. But the doctor said to wait three hours, and it's not even close. . . .

—How can you tell hunger (which demands feeding) from the need to suck (which might warrant a pacifier) or from "gas" (which calls for rest for the stomach and

would only be made worse by further feeding)?
—You hold your baby half-bent over your shoulder, or propped seated on your lap, pressing or massaging gently on the tummy, hoping to coax the troublesome "gas" bubble one way or the other—either up or down—and out. (Did you remember to have an extra diaper at the ready to shield your clothes, or were you planning to shower and change anyway—again? Do thin whitish stripes off-center down the back of your shirt seem to mix and match well enough with the rest of your wardrobe?)

Wet?

—Maybe slightly. But enough to prompt *that* cry?
—You check for undone, hurtful diaper pins, feeling a bit silly when you discover you used no pins because the diapers are the disposable type.

Cold or hot?

—Aha! You see a bluish or reddish tint to the skin. But peering closer you notice the thin blood vessels threading (normally!) blue beneath the surface, or the slight rash which you now know will disappear by tomorrow.
—You see neither shivers nor gooseflesh. You check for perspiration, feeling with your cheek or lips, since by now your own palms have grown a tad clammy.

Tired? (No, not you, your baby.)

—You were often told that babies sleep a lot, "When not eating" (or eating and eliminating), "they are sleeping" (or sleeping and eliminating). But no one seems to have impressed your baby with that notion. Your baby hasn't napped all
   —morning.

—afternoon.
—day.
—last night (yawn!).
—You pick up your baby and soon notice, through your own heavily drooping eyelids, a pair of smaller, heavily drooping eyelids. You make a choice:
  —To sleep (both of you together, holding and being held)
        or
  —Not to sleep (waiting a bit, then moving gently toward the crib, where you hope to empty your arms without having those smaller eyelids pop open, yours being in no such danger. Are small eyelids opened by the springs under crib mattresses? You make a mental note to check the fine print on the crib guarantee.)

Bored or overstimulated?

—Have you splashed bright colors around the baby's room or toned down the nest with quiet pastels? What type surroundings does your baby seem to like at what times?
—What interests your baby? Toys, mobiles, lights, the activity of the nearby shopping center, attention from other people? What about your presence? Have you fully appreciated that your face, your smile, your voice (not your words exactly, but the cadence, the tenor of your vocalizations), your scent, and your touch are probably the ultimate stimulation for your new baby?
—The presence of the familiar allows your baby to feel safe enough for change to be alerting, interesting, encouraging of experimentation and growth. You are familiar to your baby. So when you make faces, speak or sing at varying pitches, move closer and farther away (even in and out of range of vision), or adjust the position in which you are holding your baby, you provide changes which can be stimulating without being

overwhelming.

—Your baby delights at mild surprises. So you learn to signal your baby to expect you to make a certan fun sound, by opening your mouth or eyes a certain way in preparation. You let your baby watch your finger come closer and closer before it playfully taps or tickles. You repeat the action right away, doing it more or less the same way. You notice your baby seems all the more tickled because you have set up an expectation and created a mild surprise.

—And what is restful, quieting to your baby? The gentle motion of a swing, a car ride? Your rocking or snuggling with your body? The pulsing of your nearby heartbeat? The repetition of a tune? The very rhythm of sucking? A normal-for-your-household level of noise assuring that you are close by?

—Some babies simply arrive in this world easier to comfort and soothe than other babies.

—It would be interesting, and may even prove useful at times, to take a few minutes every now and again to jot down some of your observations about your baby, your interactions with your baby, and how you feel right then about your baby, yourself, your family of three. You might want to get a notebook to keep on hand for this purpose, should the spirit ever move you to take pen in hand. You'd never have to show it to anyone else if you didn't want to, you know.

This writing may seem quite unnecessary to you; after all, every ounce of this newness and growing seems so incredibly significant to you at this point that it's hard to believe you *could*, let alone, *would* ever forget any of the details. But just in case, you'll be glad to have it later. Meanwhile, the act of writing could offer a useful outlet for some feelings which might not seem all that comfortable if left bottled up inside you. This journal could also prove useful at times when you may want to compare how your baby seems to be

looking or acting this minute with how your baby usually has seemed to you. You may not always be able
to recall everything on cue, especially if you are under
some sort of stress, as you likely will be when you
come face-to-face with the final item on your list of
baby discomforts.

Sick?

—Probably not. Still, this is the possibility that could
worry you most. What if something is really wrong
and you are (neglectfully?) wasting valuable time
checking out lesser items on this list? Well, you certainly have time to take stock of all the other messages
your baby has been giving you besides this seemingly
endless crying.

—How have the day's patterns been going until now?
Has your baby shown the usual amount of interest in
being fed? Have bowel movements looked and smelled
more or less as they usually have? (Runny isn't funny,
but it's not necessarily sick, either.) Does your baby's
color, posture, or temperature seem noticeably different, strange to you? You just might want to consult
your journal if you've managed to make some entries,
to give you a clearer grasp of what you usually observe. You may want to consult your Spock-tionary, at
least see if the index lists anything to the point.

—In any event, if the overall picture your baby presents
still worries you, obviously you will consult your pediatrician. None of that you-wouldn't-want-to-bother-
the-doctor nonsense. Getting calls is an expected part
of your doctor's pediatric practice. And, just for the
record, no question ought to be considered too "silly"
or "dumb" to ask. True, most questions are not all that
pressing and can wait until your next scheduled office
visit. Some bear asking by phone between visits, but
during your doctor's regular office hours. However, if

you see signs that your baby may be unwell in some way that's unclear to you, and you are unsure of what care may be required, you'll call to ask, whatever the time. (Okay, so you'll want to avoid calling in the middle of the night whenever feasible. Still, if your own good-enough judgment tells you to call, do so in your baby's best interests. Probably you will be told nothing earth shattering. Most likely you'll learn that nothing is very wrong with your baby; that you'd probably have done about what was suggested, anyway; and that your doctor is not upset with you for calling.) But there just may be times when the most appropriate thing for you to do for your baby is to lower your own level of anxiety.

In any case, it's not just your baby's different cries to which you react. You are stimulated by your baby's non-vocal cues as well. Your baby, after all, is an active participant in your beginning relationship.

True, temperamentally, some babies are more active and some more passive. A "normal" degree of activity—like almost everything else about "normal" babies—encompasses a wide range of variations. "The Norm" is an ephemeral, theoretical, if not fictitious point in a field of possible normal points. So if you read books or talk to people that present expectations about babies' "normal" development in terms of specific weeks and months, you'll understand that you are being given only a rough idea. And if your baby falls outside the range set forth—or seems way behind (or ahead of) your sister-in-law's or neighbor's baby of the same age—you'll try to contain yourself and not get overly worried (or overly excited). If you express your concerns to your pediatrician, you may get help keeping a "normal" perspective.

Meanwhile, remind yourself that not only does "normal" development cover a wide range, but also a baby (indeed any *person*) accomplishes different kinds of developmental tasks at different rates of speed. Specifically, babies don't usually seem to do physical and verbal growing all at the same time. So your baby, who first turned over six ever-lovin' weeks later than Susie's and Jeff's kid, turns out to be the first kid on your block to say, "Dada!" Or, after sitting up so smartly even before the age your favorite "expert" listed as the early side of "normal," your baby may not say much at all before age three.

Although "normal" development, at best, shows an uneven progress, the possibility of there being some sort of true developmental problem may need to be ruled out for you to feel comfortable. (For tips on approaching your pediatrician about this, see "Who Cares About Parents, Anyway?")

At any rate, how active or passive your baby tends to be is a relative matter, a matter of degrees. No baby is absolutely passive and completely helpless, an empty vessel for you carefully to fill. This is sometimes hard to keep in mind, since, by comparison, you feel so big, so powerful; it is easy for you to exaggerate the helplessness and fragility of your infant in your own mind. In fact, your newborn arrived equipped with some critically important capacities. For example:

—Your baby will manage to turn and face to one side or the other if laid with nose pressing against something—like mattress or nipple—in order to clear passages for breathing. (Of course, while you do the feeding, you do your best to angle things—bottle, breast, baby—so that breathing continues to be no real challenge for your baby.)

—Your baby will "root" around for a satisfying nipple, turning toward whichever cheek receives the slightest stroking, especially if hungry or needing to suck. (This searching action—tiny mouth already busily at work,

opening and pursing shut, neck twisting in pursuit—
can arouse your sympathies. You may find yourself
thinking, There ought to be a quicker way to supply
the yummy nipple, be it breast, bottle, or pacifier. You
wonder at what age thumbs are discovered. Meanwhile, perhaps you can take the heat off yourself by
seeing this as a real opportunity for your baby to begin
feeling active in stimulating you—your noticing, your
understanding, and eventually your caretaking
response.)
—Your baby will create an almost adhesive suction on
the nipple with that tiny mouth. (You've actually had
to learn how to wiggle your smallest finger in between
your baby's lips in the corner of the mouth to break
the suction when you feel a burp is in order—and
your baby just keeps sucking heartily.)
—Your baby will grasp with surprising strength in those
small hands and fingers. (Just try prying your baby's
fist loose from around that handful of hair you'd really
much prefer to keep attached to your head, thank you.)
—Your baby will "startle," arms spread out protectively
in reflex, if suddenly jolted by external or internal
stimuli. (Your baby's startles during sleep prompt you
to wonder, Do babies dream? What goes on in their
sleeping or waking minds? Again, you wish yours had
words and could tell you already.)

Even newborn babies, then, are sturdier than one might
think. In fact, there may be pitfalls hidden in the belief
that babies require only the most gentle handling possible. (Might they break?) Were you to harbor such a belief, you might convey to your baby—through the way
you hold, move, bathe, touch your infant—a tentative
attitude about both your good-enough parenting and your
baby's good-enough hardiness. Rather, you want to convey to your baby a general confidence that you both will
survive, that in the most basic way, your baby is safe

enough. And your baby can sense more in your handling than you are even aware of feeling yourself, let alone communicating.

Thus, you both learn to count on the firm quality of your care. You snuggle your baby close against your solid body. Your calm, steady voice offers encouragement as you stuff a small, stiffened arm into a clean, doll-sized shirt, convinced you are not about to dislocate your baby's shoulder. At bath times, your supporting arm reaches around your baby's back and, from underneath, you grasp the small arm farthest from you—tightly enough to reassure both of you that—no matter how soapy—there is no way for that little body to slip away. You kiss your baby with enough pressure to be felt. And when you are sure your baby is tired, you put him or her down, knowing—and therefore somehow communicating to your baby—that all is well. (This brings up Dr. Winnicott again. He made the point that to allow a baby to be out of your arms can at times be the most appropriate form of "holding." He used the term *holding* in the interestingly broadened sense of meaning "whatever causes a baby—indeed, any person—to feel warm, soothed, safe." So there are sleep times when you provide "holding" by laying your baby down alone in a comfortable, supportive, and safe place to rest.)

There are, of course, times when your baby's vocal and nonvocal cues call upon you to do something other than particular caretaking tasks. In fact as the weeks pass you find your baby spending an increasing amount of time in a "quiet, alert state," inviting you to play, to interact. This interaction does not go in only one direction the way your caretaking activities do; it goes both ways. Your baby participates with you.

You and your baby respond to each other. You each observe the other responding and you encourage each other to continue the cycle of mutual involvement. Your baby's eyes track your movements, in the first days and

weeks focusing most clearly at about an eight-inch distance (which curiously approximates how close your face
would be to your baby's if in position to nurse or, typically, to bottle feed). You look into each other's eyes. Your
baby drinks you in with interest. Your eyes return the
compliment. They are a mirror, reflecting back the baby's
own feeling state and your own feelings about your baby's being lovable, "good enough." The mutuality of this
"good baby-good parent" cycle is an important happening for you but is even more essential for your baby.
How else could your baby begin to build in images of
himself or herself as a good-enough person?

Of course, you can't expect this happy cycle to be an
all-the-time pattern. You might indeed opt for that kind
of boredom, if you could, but you aren't likely to be given
such a choice. Sometimes your baby's fussing seems to
go on and on. You will have ticked through your list of
baby discomforts, and tried everything you could dream
up with no apparent result—unless you count your own
exasperation, which is an all-too-apparent result. Furthermore, if the truth be known, there are probably even
times when your baby isn't so overly fussy, but you just
feel overwhelmed and/or exhausted by all you have to
do, by all the care you need to give.

You realize you feel angry, angry at your baby. You
know, of course, that nothing is your baby's fault. (Your
baby's just being a baby.) You may feel rather horrified
at yourself for being angry at such an innocent, helpless
creature—yours, at that. How unfeeling, irrational,
nonparental, you may judge yourself to be, at least until
you have (or make) the chance to share your angry feelings with other new parents. Then you might discover
how normal and expectable this anger is at times. Perhaps it still won't feel comfortable to you. But you are
clear about the difference between feelings and actions.
You just want to be sure, deep down, that you will handle your anger in ways essentially safe for your baby.

Obviously, your anger must not spill out in grossly harmful behaviors.

Specifically, your baby will be safe if you let out your anger in words. An occasional sudden screech, coming as a more-than-mild surprise, may very well elicit a startled response from your baby. But no real damage is done. And if, exasperated, you express your anger by letting your baby cry unattended a bit longer than usual—giving yourself time and space to recoup some spent supplies of patience and energy—well, isn't that basically being protective rather than hurtful toward or neglectful of your baby?

You may not need such a "breather" to ensure your baby's physical safety but rather to protect your own good feelings about your baby, so you can go on honestly reflecting these back and preserving the "good baby-good parent" cycle.

So when you as an individual or a couple feel extra angry, or completely spent, you try to arrange for someone else to take care of your baby for a bit, to spell you while you go for a walk, or to a movie, or out to shop, or in to nap.

Maybe you can avoid getting to that point too often if you plan such "breathers" into your regular routine. It would help just to know that the next planned "breather" is to come soon. After all, it's a lot easier to feel patient with your baby's crying when you know you're going out for a quiet dinner or a visit with friends in an hour or two.

You might be better able to give yourself permission to take some regular breaks in your baby-care routine if you recognize that no one can or will replace you as a parent to your baby. Once you and your baby have begun to feel attached to each other, once the cycle of mutual responding is under way, you are your baby's mother or father, for keeps. So if you allow others to provide good-enough care while you refresh yourself with a break, you are in no way relinquishing your parenthood. In fact, interim caretakers can offer your baby specific supplements of developmental stimulation. But that's part of next chapter's story.

Growing Separate Together

It would be easy for you to collect armfuls of books and articles that detail infant development. Some of these might prove quite interesting, informative, and insightful.

It can also be overwhelming. You may have deliberately avoided all these readings, fearing it might be overwhelming to look ahead, to think too much about all of your baby's developmental happenings and what each one might mean. You may have intended to get to some of that reading but have felt overwhelmed by how much there is, unsure of what to select, and where to begin. (Do not be overwhelmed with guilt if you have done no reading of this sort. Yet you may have experienced a twinge or two, wondering if there might be something written on this subject that you really "ought" to be reading.) Or maybe you have managed to do some reading and feel overwhelmed by the intricacies and complexities of the subject—and by the lack of clarity about just where you fit into the picture, how this deeper understanding of your baby's psychological development should translate into your being a better parent.

Surely, when you think about it rationally, you see that:

—Plenty of people who have never read anything about infant development are truly good-enough parents.
—The amount you read about infants does not necessarily correlate with the amount of usable information you have, let alone with how well equipped you are to parent your baby.

151

—A lot of information can be confusing because:
  —there is so much to understand, order, and fit into
    some kind of sensible overview,
  —it is too easy to lose sight of what is really most
    important.

So this chapter will not try to duplicate or even summarize all that is written about the psychological development of infants. Rather, it will attempt:

—to present a general picture,
—to highlight the main points,
—to discuss what this picture suggests is most important about your role as a parent at each stage of your baby's progress.

Now, lest you feel overly responsible for your baby's development, you need to understand that some pre-programming has already been done. The genes which you and your partner have passed on to your baby contain the seeds of the developmental unfolding that includes psychological as well as physiological processes. The unfolding is already underway. You needn't do anything further to set it in motion. What's more, you would be hard pressed to stop the unfolding. Of course, you might be able to contribute to its going more (or less) smoothly.

To smooth the way for this unfolding you can provide a "holding" relationship that presents a minimum of snags and delays in your baby's development. Naturally, you might provide such a relationship doing no reading at all. Yet you may well be someone who likes to understand as much as possible about what is going on with the new member of your family. You may hope that your reading will offer further guidelines for you as a parent, or give you ways to check that your responses to your new baby are good enough.

For either purpose, it might help you to focus first on

your baby's most basic needs. Then, if you care to fill in details from accounts available elsewhere, you could maintain a clear, balanced overview with less danger of being overwhelmed by the further complexities. So what follows is a description of the most essential ways in which your relationship with your baby has been and will continue to be smoothing the way for developmental unfolding.

What you really need is an intimate, animated understanding of how this brand-new existence in the world seems from your baby's perspective. Can you try to imagine how it might have been for you way back when you were that tiny and new? It is difficult to picture yourself without most of your present mental capacities. The experiences of that stage are not exactly on the top of your mind, let alone on the tip of your tongue. But those earliest memory-traces still shimmer along primordial pathways in your brain, emitting flickers of empathy for your baby. It is, then, the empathy coming from your own experience that will enable you not to recall, but to imagine. . . .

And so you begin by imagining that you have just become the main character in Alice's Wonderland. You have taken a magic potion and are shrinking, getting not only smaller in size but more fetal in appearance. You curl up. You are comfortably enveloped in a warm and cozy waterbed whose spherical mattress holds you gently.

The holding offers you safety. In fact, your every need is met. Nothing at all is required of you. Just to be there. You are supplied with food and oxygen, protected from extremes of temperature and light, comforted by the constancy of a nearby two-beat pulsing, a basic iambic rhythm. Yet with all this holding you are neither needlessly restricted nor rigidly confined. Your umbilical attachment, your lifeline, is sufficiently long and flexible to allow you to float about. And should an arm or knee of yours happen to bump the curved, padded sides of your waterbed, why, the sides give way a bit in response. But you really are not aware of any of this. You are just being there.

You are too new to be able to think, but one day you may have some rudimentary perception that something is different about the way you are being held. Your waterbed has lost some of its padding. Its taut sides no longer give way easily in response to your chance collisions. Rather, they are picking up a pulsing rhythm of their own, urging you along a narrow tunnel with a light at its end. The light shines through an extraordinary keyhole that expands to allow you to tumble out. . . .

Into Wonderland. Where all is quite amazingly new. The light. The cold air. The noise. Breathing. Umbilical cord detaching. Eating. It is a strange place, this Wonderland.

You couldn't, of course, know this (or communicate as much to other Wonderlanders) but

First and foremost, you need to be helped to feel that you are still safe.

Your needs continue to be met. Your lungs fill with the necessary supply of oxygen; your mouth cries for and sucks in milk to satisfy that new physical sensation, hunger. You are unaware that you are actively participating in this intake. You are also unaware that anyone or anything aside from you is supplying milk or warmth. You have only a bodily sense of discomfort and relief from discomfort.

And since you sense sudden changes as discomfort, you are comforted by what is familiar. Any similarities between Wonderland and the world of your waterbed could help make the change more gradual, more mild. So being protected from extremes of temperature maintains a basic old-world comfort for you. Hearing or feeling the familiar iambic pulsing is a comfort, though you have no way of knowing that you are being snuggled close on the *outside* of someone's chest.

You are comforted by being held in much the same way that your waterbed enveloped you—gently, allowing you to move about as you chance to do, responding supportively but with enough "give"—an elastic, buoyant support. Rigid constraints could bruise you; needless restrictions could frustrate you; hovering confinement could smother you. But you need to sense that the sides are still close by, guaranteeing that you stay afloat and not tumble unsupported through Wonderland. You need to feel safe just to be here.

As time goes by, you grow able to see for greater distances. You learn to control your head turnings, your arm reachings, your hand graspings. You become more aware of the sides that hold you, the place that supplies nourishment and that takes away the hunger-discomfort you feel (less often now). These sides seem to you to be part of you. But sometimes they go away, outside of your increased range of vision. Then it is as though part of you is missing and after awhile you feel not-quite-whole, no longer so safe. A Tweedle Dum minus your Tweedle Dee(s). You root about in search. When you do not find that holding part, you cry. Eventually your cry seems to tweedle Dee's return, and the very reappearance of this holding part comforts you. You can resume feeling safe just being there.

In fact, when this sequence is repeated often enough, you learn that you can feel safe for a longer and longer time without your Tweedle Dee(s). But the learning remains a bit conditional. In the first few months of your life, if your cries do not bring your Dee back for as long as a couple of days, your feeling of safety fades away along with your image of your Dee. (Even when you are as old as two years, a two-week absence of your Dee can threaten your sense that Wonderland is a safe place for you.)

You can be kept fed and dry and clean and even held

by the Dee-type person who is filling in for your true Dee(s); the ordinarily good-enough substitute can even know enough to try to keep your image of your true Dee alive and well for you—talking about your Dee, reminding you that Dee will come back to you. Still your picture of your Dee needs frequent in-person renewal to stay vivid enough for you to recall it at will. And if your Dee image fades too much, you are thrown backwards into a tumble-down world, a risky place to be.

If you avoid these too-long stretches of Dee-loss, you learn to tolerate Dee's absences and still hold on to your image of your Dee(s). And you begin to sense that Dee is not exactly a part of you, after all. You are learning some crucially important things about yourself:

—Dee(s) can disappear temporarily without being lost to you forever.
—You are capable of being comforted, feeling complete and safe for quite some time in Dee's absence.
—In Dee's absence you can receive nourishment and holding by some other Dee-type—preferably a familiar substitute who is capable of being responsive to your needs.

Now you begin to see others around you either as "good" Dee-types (familiars who bring comfort to you) or as "bad" non-Dees (strangers who bring discomfort, since you feel anxious if any non-Dee even comes near you). You are trying to order your world, divide it into clear categories, preserve the goodness of the Dees by isolating all "bad" in the unfamiliar non-Dees.

Meanwhile, you need to feel that the Dees see you, too, as essentially good. Otherwise, how could you feel sure that they would want to keep coming around to nourish and hold you? You sense their good feelings about you, their approval as they find you pleasing and good. You sense this mainly because the Dees accommodate their responses to your cues. Their approval of you feels all warm and cozy. Rather remarkably like the embrace of your waterbed.

> *But now you require more than a feeling that you are physically safe. You need the kind of holding which conveys to you that you are lovable and that (in a general way) it is good for you just to be where you are, who you are.*

Your Dees need to convey this message to you again and again, for you have as yet no conscious memory. In fact, the message needs to be built in as your memory is developing. The message also bears repeating because you are a developing, changing person, thirsty for feedback that the changes are appreciated. So you look for the feedback to come in many different forms:

—in gentle firmness of touch and holding,
—in maintained interest of eye contact,
—in calm and soothing, delighted and admiring tones of voice,
—in genuine smiles of shared pleasure and approval.

Approval from one so all-powerful and all-knowing as Dee seems to surely mean you are indeed worthwhile. This good feeling about yourself is so nice and necessary that after your Dee has repeated the message often enough, you find yourself keeping the feeling even when Dee goes away for awhile. It is in fact very like the smile of the Cheshire cat, which lingers brightly on long after its wearer has disappeared from view. If you can only absorb enough of the smile of approval so it remains indelibly in your memory, you can bring back the good feelings about yourself even in your Dee's absence.

Once this happens, feeling yourself held becomes a less constant need for you. Of course, you cannot appreciate the irony unfolding here, but it will continue to show up in the later stages of your development as well. The irony is that the more successful the *attachment* you have made to one or more Dees, the better are your chances of being able to achieve an adaptive *separation* from your Dee(s).

Attachment is essential in allowing you to feel safe and in helping you begin to feel worthwhile. But, eventually, you will need to separate in order to experience yourself as a whole person, an individual in your own right. And, oddly enough, attachment makes separation possible. In fact, attaching turns out to be basically for the purpose of separating.

Obviously, the irony escapes you as it unfolds. Even if as you grow up you were capable of such sophisticated thinking, even if you could come to such an objective point of view, you still would not be in a particularly favorable position for observing the irony. For this separating is, at best, a very gradual affair. It is a weaning.

Separation is a story that, as Lewis Carroll would say, "you begin at the beginning and go on till you come to an end; then stop." The story has a continuous thread which, were the end not specifically ordained, might spin on forever. The story may not seem to make a great deal of sense on its surface. But development is occurring. You, as the main character, are growing up, growing separate. But this best happens gradually.

You need to be weaned from that original attachment in which you experience your Dee as part of you. And weaning should be a gradual process, offering appropriate substitutes along the way—a cup of milk instead of a bottle or breast, and at first for only some of the feedings. So, too, the original attachment requires some sort of temporary replacement—a special blanket, perhaps, a teddy bear, even a particular bedtime ritual might do. It is, for now, part of you. It has, as a matter of fact, a singular advantage over your Dee: You can tweedle your blanket or bear any way you like. It will not go away: It will not even frown with disapproval.

You may hang on to this substitute quite tightly while

you eventually try to separate more actively from your Dees by shouting "No!" at every opportunity. "No" is your way of summing up the developmental urges you feel to be a separate person, an individual. It becomes your one-word, foot-stamping way of emphasizing to your world, to yourself, that you are you . . . that you are someone with your own wishes, quite apart from anyone else's wishes for you. "No" is such a wonderful and useful word, such a full and action-packed idea, that you like to say it just as often as you can. Of course, your Dees often seem not to like your no. And, oddly enough, you don't *want* them to like it. That's part of the point. "No" is your cry for opposition. It is a sort of sonar probe which you bounce off others in order to define the limits of you, where you begin and stop, the clear boundary between you and your Dees.

So you need your Dees to hang in there, to hold you in a new way now. You are really saying "No!-but-don't-go!"

You need someone to oppose, someone else right close by who is resilient enough to withstand your nos and not back off. The opposition permits you to begin defining yourself.

The psychological processes of separation can only occur at your pace. In fact, your development in general unfolds according to some internal clock that is specific to you. So *your* timing is the crucial factor. You are in the lead for this dance. You want your Dees to keep up, stay abreast of your changing emotional steps and patterns.

Maybe, though, you would like to know that your Dees miss your earlier patterns, the dances you used to do. That would mean that it really was okay for you to have been able to do only those simpler steps that seemed quite the rage last month. It would be nice to know, for example, that your Dees had no need for you to do the crawl instead of the scootch, so your swinging into this new movement now means that you really are leading the way. Besides, you never know when you may want to return to those simpler motions to rest up before tackling the next, more complex two-steps.

But surely you want your Dees to marvel at how you have grown, noting that the growing comes from within you, and your Dees neither push nor pull you from one dance to the next. In your Wonderland it certainly would be distracting, if not downright annoying, to have some White Rabbit racing around with his stop watch and moaning about how late it has become. You need no one heralding what is about to happen or self-importantly trying to manage everything and speed the action along. You would only become frustrated were you pushed to follow the tracks or tempo of someone else.

You need your own developmental pace to be respected.

Your emotional growth can't be rushed any more than your physical growth can be. The sequence of psychological steps you take can be predicted but just when, at what month, you take each step cannot be either known ahead of time or ordained by others. Moreover, each of your steps feels a bit shaky and tentative for awhile. Often you need to toddle backwards a bit to catch your balance before going on. You can't realize what a challenge this uneven progress of yours presents for your Dees as they attempt to keep abreast.

There is so much more to this Wonderland that your baby lives in. You really have imagined only the beginnings. But these offer challenges enough. So if, indeed, you are to respect the developmental pace of your new baby, you do not want to dash too far ahead in your imaginings.

Instead, you now may want to toddle backwards from time to time yourself, and retrace your own steps, hoping to make what you've learned as a new parent feel somewhat less shaky and tentative:

—First, you give your baby a sense of physical safety.
—Second, you hold your baby with acceptance and admiration, knowing and communicating that in a basic way you find your baby lovable, good enough just to be there.
—Third, you recall that, ironically, attachment to your baby makes separation possible for the baby later on.
—Fourth, you keep in mind that, in general terms, normal human psychological development is the story of increasing separation, of requiring an ever-roomier waterbed, of becoming more individual.
—Fifth, you understand your baby's opposition to you not as rejection but as initial attempts to discover who's who, to define a self; and so you remain available with all your parenthood, your own boundaries of self, your reasonable limits.
—Sixth, you appreciate that your baby's development is unpredictable in its timing, uneven in its flow, and you try to keep in touch, clear about how difficult this is at times for every parent.

In your own development as a parent, you may feel that you have particular difficulties toddling through one or more of these six main points, putting this learning into actual practice. Well, your parenting and your baby are rather new and will continue to offer surprises. Just prepare yourself by securing every available support, so you can cushion your family's tumble through Wonderland.

Carry On!

Someone once said, "Growing up is so hard, it should never be expected of children." Indeed, it is quite astounding to think about all that your baby has to learn—including the many things that adults take for granted, like how to move purposefully, how to predict that things will fall downward, how to make sense of the comings and goings of others.

It is also quite astounding how much you have already learned, both about yourself as a new parent and about your baby. You are increasing your awareness of and respect for all three sets of needs in your new family:

> —*Your needs as an individual;*
> —*your needs as a couple;*
> —*and your baby's needs.*

You have learned to look for and disarm cultural and personal myths so that they have less power to disrupt your good-enough parenting and your sense of yourself (and your partner) as good-enough people.

You have learned a great deal about what your baby needs and the signals your baby gives to tell you about those needs without the help of words. You can pick up many of your baby's cues and can tolerate the necessarily imperfect trial-and-error manner in which you respond. You even know enough now to expect that, just when the messages seem crystal clear to you, your baby's cues will often turn surprisingly unfamiliar. Ah-ha! you remind yourself, your baby is growing, going through some apparently sudden developmental changes, and giving

162

you new, confounding clues. You recognize that the process of your learning requires that you give yourself time
to make sense of the new clues. Since there is no way
for you immediately and automatically to learn what they
mean and how you should respond, you are patient with
yourself in catching up with your child's latest
developments.

Meanwhile, you have already learned that your baby
is remarkably tuned in to you. The umbilical cord has
been replaced by emotional attachments, hotlines for the
transmission of feelings. This transmission occurs so automatically through your body's signals that your baby
can experience discomfort when you are tense or upset
or distracted or angry. You have come to realize, then,
that it is important for you to be aware of your own emotional state, to know how you are feeling and what might
be bothering you at any given time. Taking care of yourself is an essential part of taking care of your baby. The
baby-parent dividing lines are somewhat blurry during
infancy. What is helpful to you filters through to ease
tensions in your baby. So you can see that when you feel
actively supported by your partner, or otherwise soothed
or comforted, you will inevitably transmit more support,
reassurance, and comfort to your baby.

And you are learning to make peace with the rather
indirect nature of nurture. You and your partner have
provided your baby with a full complement of designer
genes (even a name you can count on); but you realize
that you must wait for the potentials tucked away in these
genes to unfold. You may still wish you could teach your
baby what he or she must learn; you may still feel a bit
frustrated that you are making too indirect an impact for
all the hard work, long hours, and loving care you are
investing. But you temper your frustrations with your
knowledge that "good-enough" parenting is not an intrusive force-feeding of lessons and expectations. It is an
active availability, a supportive but flexible holding, a

readiness to learn to respond to whatever cues may be given.

Learning will be a continuing process for you as a parent. And, indirectly, you are beginning to teach your child by your own example. Your patience with yourself, your ability to tolerate the frustration of your own mistakes, will help prepare your child for the complicated tasks and trial-and-error efforts that his or her own learning will require.

So you "carry on!" as a good-enough parent. And you support your baby's growing up as a good-enough child.

Five New-Parent Couples
(Introduced in Chapter Seven)

Couple	Age	Birth Order	No. Marriage	Previous Pregnancy	Length Current Relationship; Length Marriage	Occupation	Baby's Sex, Age	Nursing
Barb	26	1st Dau.	1st	—	2 Yrs., 10 Mos.	Bus.-Related Professional	F 10 Wks.	No
Bob	30	2nd Son	1st	—	2 Yrs.	Physician		
Cathy	29	1st Dau.	1st	—	16 Yrs. 7½ Yrs.	Social Workers	F 7 Wks.	Yes
Curt	31	Only Child	1st	—				
Deirdre	33	1st Dau.	2nd	—	4 Yrs. 1 Yr.	Psychologist	F 5½ Wks.	Yes
Dan	37	2nd Son	2nd	Son, 10, Lives Away		Psychiatrist		
Erin	34	1st Dau.	2nd	—	2 Yrs. 4 Mos.	Restaurant Owners	F 8 Wks.	Yes
Ed	24	1st Son	1st	—				
Fern	33	1st Dau.	2nd	Premarital Abortion: Medically Necessary	3½ Yrs. 1½ Yrs.	Bus.-Related Professionals	M 8 Wks.	Yes
Frank	35	1st Son	1st					
	Age Ranges of Mothers: 26-34 Fathers: 24-37			First Baby of Each Couple	Range of Current Relationship: 2-16 Yrs. Range of Marital Relationship: 4 Mos.-7½ Yrs.	Middle Class	Age Range: 5½-10 Wks.